Sunset SALAD BOOK

Illustrations by Earl Thollander

Sunset
SALAD BOOK

By the editors of Sunset Books and Sunset Magazine

LANE BOOK COMPANY   MENLO PARK, CALIFORNIA

Library of Congress Catalog Card 62-11826

First Printing April 1962

Copyright© 1962
Lane Book Company, Menlo Park, California

Designed by Adrian Wilson

Composition by Griffin Brothers Inc.
Types: Linotype Times Roman and handset Times Italic

Paper: Antique offset book paper by Northwest Paper Company

Lithographed in the United States of America by Phillips & Van Orden Company
Binding by Phillips & Van Orden and Cardoza Bookbinding Company

Contents

THE ART OF
SALAD MAKING

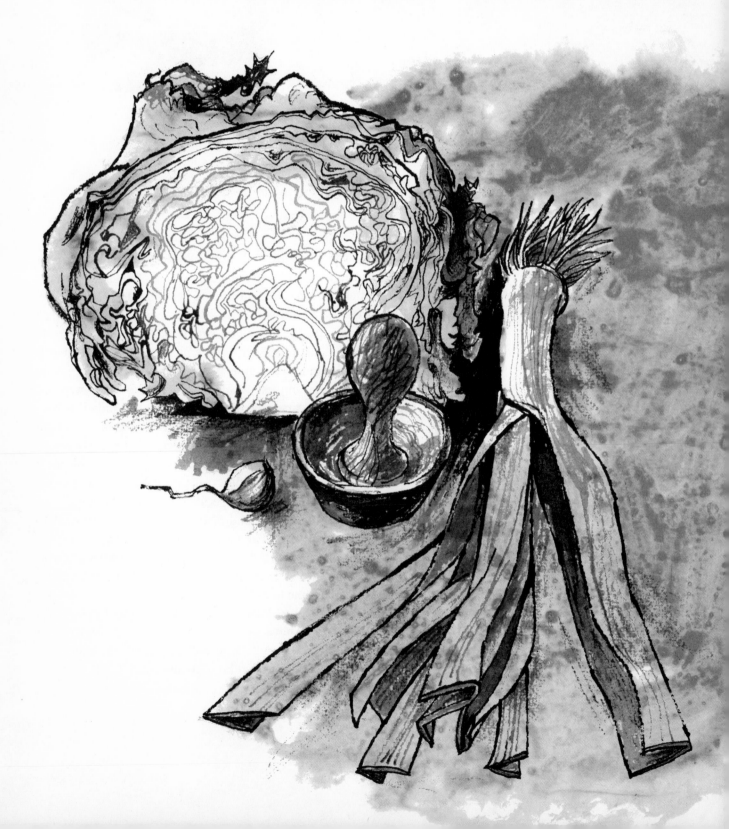

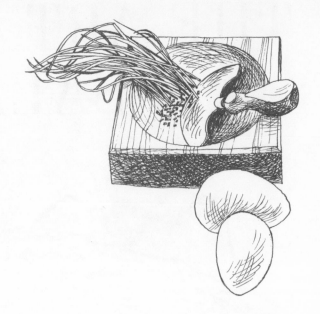

Distinctive Salads

can bring new zest and excitement to your everyday meals and new glamor to your party menus. Salads take many different forms. Each one is a personal design which reflects the inventive genius of the cook. A salad may be light or hearty. It may be simple or complex. It may be served as the introduction to a meal, as the highlight of a meal, as an accompaniment, or even as the perfect finale.

Even the simplest of salads, however, must be prepared with loving care and careful attention to details if it is to be a success. It must be appetizing to look at and a delight to the palate. A simple tossed green salad is a gourmet's favorite, but simple as it may appear, it is by no means a haphazard creation. The greens must be fresh and crisp. The dressing must be a perfect blend of seasonings, selected to make the salad distinctive and to appropriately complement the meal with which it is served.

The recipes in this book include classic salads, variations of old favorites, and many new and unusual recipes that have come to us from the kitchens of ingenious cooks. All of the recipes have been thoroughly tested in our own kitchens and have received the enthusiastic approval of our own taste panels. You will probably find many that you will want to use without change, and others that you will want to adapt to your own and your family's tastes. We hope you will be inspired to experiment.

Use salads to bring variety into your meals. If your green salads have developed a monotonous sameness, introduce new flavor accents. Try different salad greens; there are many in today's markets, and you may find a new favorite among one of the more unusual ones that you have not tried before. Try different vinegars, or combinations of vinegars. Use herbs, fresh or dried, to transform your salads and give them delicious new overtones.

By changing one or two ingredients in a salad recipe, you can give it an entirely new pattern. Suppose, for example, you eliminate the anchovies in Caesar Salad and substitute slivered salami. The salad is brand new and equally exciting. If you omit the blue cheese in a salad dressing and put some grated Parmesan cheese in its place, the whole character of the salad changes. Substitute lobster or chicken for crab or shrimp in a full-meal salad, and you have a completely new design for dining.

You'll find many inspirations for party salads here. A shimmering molded salad could be a spectacular centerpiece salad for your next party buffet. Try serving a small, tangy seafood salad to pique appetites before a meal. Or finish off a meal with a delicate frozen treat.

Salads take on excitement when they are served in eye-catching containers. There are many festive ways in which to present them. Fruits are gloriously tempting when their rainbow colors are displayed on a handsome platter or on individual serving plates. Use imagination in preparing and combining them. Group colors attractively; combine slices, chunks, halved fruits, whole berries or grapes. Garnish the arrangement with a frilly bit of curly endive or perky springs of mint or water cress, and pass the dressing separately.

Orange, grapefruit, and melon halves make ideal serving baskets—and pineapple shells can be prepared in several dramatic ways. Seafood salads become glamorous when they are heaped into lobster or crab shells. A handsome shallow bowl sets off color-bright, chilled vegetables.

Casseroles are ideal serving containers for many types of salads. The robust salads that accompany a barbecue meal are especially suited to this type of service, as are almost any of the hearty salads that replace a vegetable or an oven-baked casserole.

Garnishes give a salad its finished look. Give them special attention. A garnish can be as simple as a sprinkling of coconut, a wisp of parsley, or a topping of chopped nut meats. But it is important to the final picture. It makes a salad gay and irresistible, and it says that this salad was fun to make, fun to serve, and that it will be a delightfully flavorful taste treat.

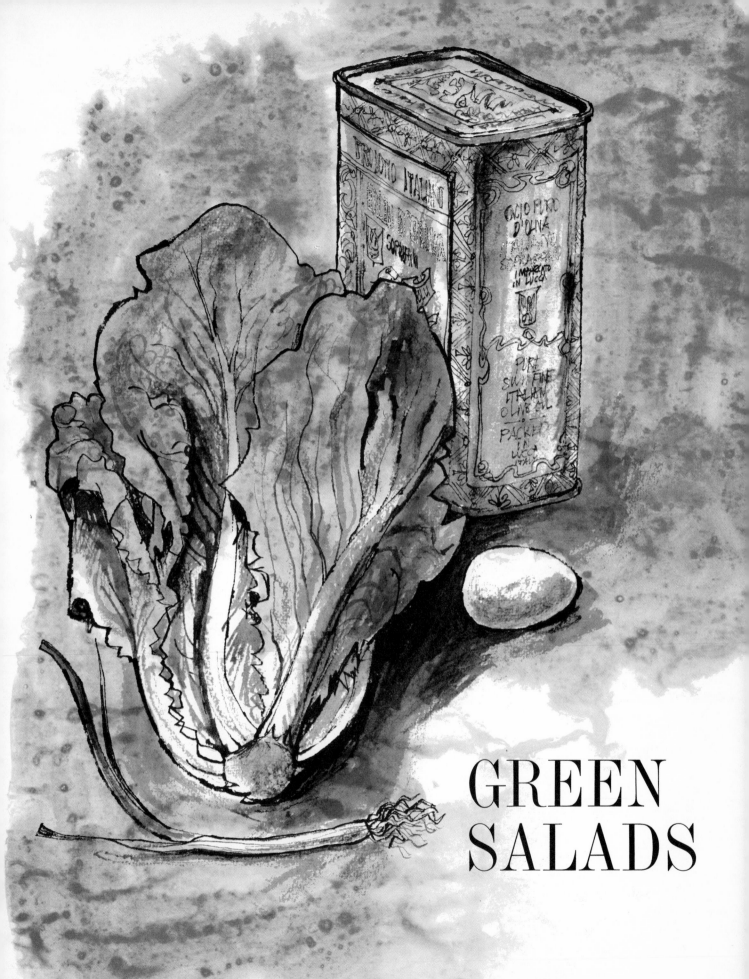

GREEN
SALADS

A Green Salad

properly prepared, is an exciting addition to a meal; lack of loving care in its preparation usually results only in uninteresting mediocrity. Since no type of salad is at home in more menus than this versatile favorite, it deserves special consideration.

A tempting array of greens is displayed in today's markets, and in the summertime you can enjoy choice, freshly picked salad ingredients from your own garden. You can choose from slender, dark green romaine, crisp head lettuce, curly endive, waxen French endive, velvety butter lettuce, spicy water cress. A green salad may be limited to just one kind, or it may be a combination of several kinds which complement each other in flavor, texture, and color. Some of the most popular salad greens, and some of the "accessory" greens which add zest and individuality to a green salad, are shown in photographs on pages 134 and 135 of this book.

The same rules hold true for preparing all types of salad greens. Always handle them very tenderly so they won't bruise. It's best to wash greens the day before you plan to serve them, so they can chill and crisp. Wash them quickly but thoroughly in running water; remove wilted leaves, but do not separate the heads. Stand them upside down to drain (not more than 30 minutes). Shake off the remaining excess moisture by gently tossing the greens in a clean towel or by shaking them in a wire lettuce basket. Put greens into the crisper section of your refrigerator, or in a plastic bag. When serving time comes, pat off any moisture left on the leaves. Tear the lettuce into bite-size pieces just before serving. (If you're making salad for a large group, you might tear the leaves an hour ahead and store them in large plastic bags in the refrigerator.)

Often you can add individuality to a green salad by choosing a special dressing that has a strong character of its own. The Caesar Salad and the Green Goddess Salad (both on page 20), are examples of the green salad that features a special dressing. However, the most popular dressing for greens is the true French type, made of 3 parts oil to 1 part vinegar or lemon juice, with seasonings to taste. This is the basic formula, but it is capable of many variations of flavor. Some salad makers prefer the proportion of 2 parts oil to 1 part vinegar. The vinegar may be wine vinegar, cider vinegar, one of the herb-flavored vinegars, or a combination of vinegars. Some people like sugar in a French dressing; others do not. Seasonings may include such ingredients as curry, paprika, Tabasco, soy, Worcestershire, and fresh or dried herbs. Green salad enthusiasts do agree on one point, however—the delicate "bite" of freshly ground, coarse black pepper gives a green salad the zip and zest that it needs.

Strictly speaking, a green salad consists only of greens and a carefully seasoned dressing. If you add other ingredients, regard them merely as accessories; never let them dominate. Some additions that have special value because of flavor or texture are chopped water chestnuts, green or ripe olives, capers, minced herbs, and toasted sesame or caraway seeds, either sprinkled on top or tossed with the greens and dressing.

Fruits and vegetables, either raw or cooked, may be added to a green salad to give it a seasonal touch. The list is endless—tomatoes, sweet onion, green pepper, radishes, diced avocado, and cucumbers are some of the most common. For more unusual additions, try raw or slightly cooked asparagus tips, sliced raw or cooked mushrooms, artichoke hearts, grated raw beets, hearts of palm, seedless grapes, or sliced apple.

Green Salad, Smörgåsbord Style

The idea here is simple: bringing the greens, the "go-alongs," and the Piquant Dressing (page 125) to the table in separate containers. The dressing is added, the greens are mixed and served into individual bowls, then guests help themeslves to a selection of the other ingredients. In the picture on page 137, we used equal parts of romaine, leaf, and Australian lettuce, with small amounts of Belgian endive and chicory. We also had pitted ripe olives, stuffed with sticks of jack cheese; avocado cubes; halved artichoke hearts (preserved in oil); fresh mushroom slices; green onion pieces, feathered on each end; crumbled crisp bacon combined with halved toasted filberts.

You can use any favorite selection of greens that will give a good balance of color, flavor, and texture. And you can vary the additions with such things as toasted sesame seeds, shredded Parmesan cheese, sliced water chestnuts or almonds, thin slices of apple, thin lemon curls, smoked oysters, bean sprouts, or croutons.

Bring in the crisp, cold greens, kept separate in a large bowl. Bring the other ingredients to the table in wooden bowls or whatever looks best with your table setting—perhaps small abalone shells, Japanese rice bowls (or their covers), even large-sized dinner wine glasses.

Basic Green Salad

Wash a head of leafy lettuce (or an assortment of greens) quickly and gently in cold water. Shake very well, then pat dry with cloth or paper towels. Put into a crisping pan or plastic bag and refrigerate. At the last minute, tear lettuce into bite-size pieces into salad bowl.

Put a teaspoon of salt in the bottom of a large wooden bowl. Skin a clove of garlic (a fresh clove will skin easily after it is hit briskly with a knife handle). Hold the garlic between your thumb and forefinger and grind it on the salt until half the clove is gone; discard the remainder. Add a sprinkle of seasoning salt to taste (or individual herbs of your choice). Add the lettuce to the bowl and pour over 2 tablespoons olive oil. Toss gently until all the leaves are coated. Grind pepper over the lettuce, to taste, and then add 2 teaspoons shallot-flavored wine vinegar. Toss lightly. Makes about 4 servings.

Spinach and Egg Salad

1 hard-cooked egg
1 clove garlic
¼ teaspoon each dry mustard
and pepper
½ teaspoon paprika
1 teaspoon salt
¼ cup vinegar
½ cup salad oil
2 tablespoons chopped parsley
1 small onion, thinly sliced
½ pound fresh spinach
½ head lettuce

Crisp, dark green, slightly spicy spinach gives lettuce a sharp accent in this salad dressed with vinegar, oil, and well-selected seasonings. Thinly sliced green onions could be substituted for the dry onion.

Separate egg yolk from white and drop egg yolk into a salad bowl which has been rubbed with the cut clove of garlic; mash yolk with a wooden spoon. Add the seasonings, then stir in the vinegar and oil. Chop egg white and mix in with the parsley. Add sliced onion and the raw spinach and lettuce which have been torn into bite-size pieces. Toss lightly. Makes 4 generous servings.

Frosted Lettuce Wedges

1 teaspoon chili powder
½ teaspoon water
1 cup mayonnaise
1 can (6 oz.) tomato paste
1 teaspoon garlic salt
1 large head of lettuce

Garlic salt picks up the individual flavors in the creamy dressing that frosts these lettuce wedges.

Dissolve chili powder in water, then stir into mayonnaise along with tomato paste and garlic salt. Beat until smooth, then let stand 30 minutes. Cut lettuce in 8 wedges; frost with dressing just before serving. Makes 8 servings.

Spinach and Tomato Salad

Tear 1 small bunch of spinach into small pieces. Halve about 10 cherry tomatoes; toss with the spinach; toss with French dressing just before serving. Serves 2.

Lemon Lettuce

4 tablespoons (¼ cup) lemon juice
4 tablespoons (¼ cup) sugar
1 small head of lettuce

Lemon and sugar are good foils for the blandness of head lettuce. We suggest you serve it with fish or wild game.

Pour lemon juice over sugar and let stand 2 hours. Stir mixture occasionally so it becomes syrupy. Trim lettuce, remove core, then break into chunks or cut into wedges. Spoon lemon dressing over lettuce just before serving. Makes 4 servings.

Fascination Salad

8 slices bacon, cut in ½-inch pieces
1 medium-sized head of lettuce
¼ cup chopped green onion (including some of the tops)
2 hard-cooked eggs, sliced

The fascinating thing about this salad is that in spite of the hot bacon-flavored dressing, the lettuce retains its crispness.

Fry the bacon until crisp and browned. Drain, and use the drippings in making the dressing (recipe below). Break lettuce into bite-size pieces in a salad bowl. Add green onion and hard-cooked egg slices. Pour over the bacon dressing, tossing lightly. Serve immediately. Makes 6 to 8 servings.

BACON DRESSING:
Measure ¼ cup of the bacon drippings, and put back into frying pan. Add 3 tablespoons vinegar or lemon juice; 1 teaspoon sugar; ½ teaspoon *each* paprika, dry mustard, and salt; and a dash of pepper. Stir over low heat until hot.

Green Salad with Cucumber and Buttermilk Dressing

⅓ cup buttermilk
2 tablespoons mayonnaise
2 tablespoons lemon juice
½ teaspoon dill weed
½ teaspoon salt
Freshly ground pepper
½ cucumber (about a 4-inch section), finely diced
4 to 6 cups broken pieces crisp head lettuce

Shake together all ingredients except lettuce pieces. Pour over lettuce and toss lightly. Makes 4 servings.

Spinach Greens Salad with Pine Nut Dressing

½ cup chopped pine nuts
¼ cup salad or olive oil
3 tablespoons tarragon vinegar
¼ teaspoon grated lemon peel
½ teaspoon salt
Dash nutmeg
1½ quarts broken pieces crisp, fresh spinach

Combine pine nuts, salad or olive oil, vinegar, lemon peel, salt, and nutmeg. Toss with spinach. Makes 6 servings.

Egg and Olive Lettuce Salad

1 head lettuce
2 hard-cooked eggs
2 tablespoons chopped ripe olives
2 tablespoons diced green pepper
1 tablespoon finely cut chives
¾ cup salad oil
¼ cup mild vinegar or lemon juice
1 tablespoon sugar
1 teaspoon each salt, paprika, and
dry mustard
¼ teaspoon pepper
Few drops liquid onion or garlic

Break lettuce into bite-size pieces in a salad bowl. Press eggs through a fine sieve. Add eggs, olives, green pepper, and chives to lettuce. To make dressing, combine remaining ingredients and shake or mix well. Add dressing to taste. Toss lightly and serve. Makes about 5 servings.

Spanish Salad

1 large clove garlic
3 slices French bread, toasted
3 hard-cooked eggs
1 head lettuce or romaine
½ cup minced ripe olives
French dressing or mayonnaise

Rub garlic on slices of toasted French bread; cut toast into small cubes or tear into small pieces. Chop eggs finely, tear lettuce into bite-size pieces. Combine toast cubes, chopped eggs, minced olives, and lettuce, and toss with French dressing or mayonnaise. Makes 6 servings.

Creamy Lettuce Salad

2 small heads of lettuce
or 2 quarts of leaf lettuce
6 slices bacon
1 tablespoon flour
1 cup (½ pint) commercial
sour cream
2 tablespoons vinegar
2 teaspoons sugar
1 teaspoon salt

For luncheon you might serve this salad with rye bread and cheese sandwiches. As a dinner salad, its flavor would go well with steak, lamb chops, or fried chicken.

Wash the lettuce and drain well; break into a large salad bowl. Cut the bacon into small pieces and fry until crisp and browned. Add flour to the bacon and drippings, and stir over low heat until flour is well blended. Add sour cream, vinegar, sugar, and salt; stir constantly until mixture is a smooth, thin sauce. Pour over the lettuce. Toss lightly and serve at once. Makes 6 to 8 servings when used as a dinner salad.

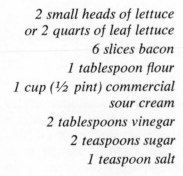

Antipasto Salad

Anyone who has eaten in Italian restaurants is familiar with *antipasto*—those tempting morsels of such foods as salami, cheese, pickled vegetables, and anchovies that Italians traditionally serve as appetizers. We suggest that you combine some of these piquantly flavored foods in a typical, first course, green salad. We tried various combinations for "antipasto salads" and found all delicious.

The basic plan of an antipasto salad is simple. You just arrange a bed of greens in your salad bowl, then top the greens with a colorful array of any of the foods you might find on a tray of antipasto. Bring it to the table untossed, to show off the colorful arrangement; then mix with a simple oil and wine vinegar dressing. The result: a robust, first course salad for a summer dinner or a main dish salad to serve with a hot bread for lunch or a light supper.

For the greens, choose romaine, escarole, leaf lettuce, or head lettuce; add a bit of chicory or dandelion greens, if available, for the sharp, bitter tang they contribute. Tear the greens into bite-sized pieces as you would for a regular green salad, or shred them. Either way, make a bed of crisp greens in a well-chilled salad bowl.

Let your imagination, your sense of flavor and color, and the contents of your kitchen dictate the assortment you choose for the antipasto toppings: canned tuna, drained and broken in chunks; anchovy fillets, rolled or plain; green or ripe olives, chopped or sliced; hard-cooked eggs, chopped or sliced; salami, shredded or cut in pieces; radish slices; green pepper, chopped or sliced; minced parsley; pimiento strips; chopped green onions; pickled artichoke hearts, halved or quartered; pickled mushrooms, sliced; Italian pickled vegetables, drained and chopped; fresh tomatoes, chopped or cut in wedges and seeded. When you've made your choice, arrange the foods attractively on the greens.

DRESSING:

To blend the hearty flavors of an antipasto salad, a very plain oil and vinegar dressing is best. We suggest 1 part red wine vinegar with 3 parts mild olive oil (this may be part salad oil). Use garlic-flavored vinegar or oil if you wish, or rub the salad bowl with a cut clove of garlic before you begin. Add dressing and toss salad just before serving.

Stuffed Hearts of Lettuce

Select 2 medium-sized, well-formed heads of iceberg lettuce (they should be green and rather loose). Remove loose outer leaves; core. Run cold water into core to loosen head; drain very thoroughly. Make dressing by whirling in a blender or electric mixer, until smooth, 1 cup *each* sour cream and mayonnaise and 4 ounces crumbled blue cheese. Slowly pour dressing into cored part and between leaves of lettuce heads, so lettuce absorbs as much dressing as possible. Wrap heads in waxed paper or clean, damp towels. Chill in vegetable compartment of refrigerator 6 hours or until dressing is firm. Cut heads in quarter wedges. Serve immediately. Makes 8 servings.

Syrian Spinach Salad

1 pound fresh spinach
1 teaspoon salt
4 green onions, finely sliced
2 tablespoons each lemon juice
and olive oil
½ cup chopped salted pecans

Chopped salted pecans give a totally new character to raw spinach salad, dressed simply with lemon juice and olive oil.

Wash spinach thoroughly and cut off coarse stems and roots. Drain well and shake to remove excess moisture. Chop coarsely and turn into a shallow pan. Sprinkle with salt and roll and toss spinach in your hands; then squeeze dry. Turn into a salad bowl; add onions, lemon juice, and olive oil, and toss lightly. Sprinkle with nut meats. Makes 4 servings.

Spinach and Bacon Salad

2 pounds fresh spinach
2 heads red leaf lettuce
or 1 head iceberg lettuce
½ pound bacon
¼ cup sugar
1 teaspoon each salt
and dry mustard
1 tablespoon juice scraped
from onion
⅓ cup cider vinegar
1 cup salad oil
1 tablespoon poppy seed (optional)
1½ cups large curd cottage cheese

We recommend this crisp, green salad for both its flavor and appearance. The thin, tangy dressing is slightly sweet, so you may prefer to serve the salad European style—as a separate course after the meat.

Thoroughly wash and drain the spinach; break off stems and tear apart large leaves. Combine with the lettuce, broken in bite-size pieces. Fry bacon until crisp; then cool, crumble it, and add to greens. For the dressing, combine the sugar, salt, mustard, onion juice, vinegar, and salad oil. Shake or beat well. Add poppy seeds, if used, and shake again. Use about half of this dressing to toss in the greens. Add cottage cheese to remaining dressing; toss with salad greens. Makes 8 servings.

1 clove garlic
¾ cup olive oil or salad oil
2 cups croutons
2 large heads romaine
½ teaspoon salt
Freshly ground pepper
2 eggs, cooked 1 minute
Juice of 1 large lemon
6 to 8 anchovy fillets, chopped
½ cup grated Parmesan cheese

Caesar Salad is invariably tossed at the table, where everyone can watch the host or hostess season and mix the greens and drop in each additional ingredient—eggs, anchovies, cheese, and croutons—with a flourish.

Crush garlic in a small bowl, pour over the oil, and let stand several hours. Brown the croutons (preferably made from stale sourdough French bread) in ¼ cup of the garlic oil, stirring often. (If you prefer, you can toast the bread cubes in a slow oven.) Tear romaine into a large salad bowl, sprinkle with salt, and grind over a generous amount of pepper. Pour over remaining garlic oil and toss until every leaf is glossy.

Break the 1-minute eggs into salad; squeeze over the lemon juice, and toss thoroughly. Add chopped anchovies and grated cheese, and toss again. Lastly, add the croutons, toss gently, and serve immediately. Makes about 12 servings.

Green Goddess Salad

8 to 10 anchovy fillets
1 green onion
¼ cup minced parsley
2 tablespoons minced fresh tarragon or 1 tablespoon dried tarragon soaked in vinegar and then strained
¼ cup finely cut chives
3 cups mayonnaise
¼ cup tarragon vinegar
1 clove garlic
1 large head romaine
1 pound cooked lobster, shrimp, crab meat, or chicken

This famous salad was first created in 1915 at the Palace Hotel in honor of George Arliss, who was appearing in San Francisco that year in William Archer's play, "The Green Goddess." There are many variations to this creamy dressing. Some cooks use sour cream for part of the mayonnaise or anchovy paste instead of the fish fillets. Others use a blender to chop together the parsley, tarragon, chives, and anchovy fillets. Well-seasoned French dressings may be used instead of the vinegar.

Chop together the anchovies and green onion until finely minced. Add parsley, tarragon, and chives, and mix lightly. Turn into a bowl and stir in mayonnaise and vinegar, mixing well. Rub a salad bowl with 1 cut clove of garlic and break romaine into bite-size pieces into the bowl.

Pour over enough dressing to moisten (about 2 cups), toss lightly, spoon on salad plates, and garnish with desired shellfish or chicken. Makes 6 servings. Recipe makes about 1 quart dressing, or enough for 12 servings. (You can store the leftover dressing in a covered container in the refrigerator for at least a week.)

Summer Salad

2 cups finely sliced fresh spinach
1½ cups sliced peeled cucumbers
⅓ cup sliced green onions,
  including some of the tops
½ cup sliced radishes
1 pint (2 cups) creamed cottage
  cheese
1 cup commercial sour cream
2 teaspoons lemon juice
½ teaspoon salt
Freshly ground pepper
Parsley and paprika for garnish

This crisp green salad serves well in all situations—as a light lunch, a first course, an accompaniment for a dinner or supper menu.

In a bowl combine sliced spinach, sliced cucumbers, onions, and radishes; toss together lightly. Arrange on 4 individual salad plates or in wooden salad bowls. In center of each serving, place a mound of cottage cheese. Blend together sour cream, lemon juice, salt, and pepper, and pour over salads. Sprinkle top of each salad with a little paprika and chopped parsley. Makes 4 servings.

Chef's Salad

4 to 6 slices bacon
4 to 6 cups torn salad greens
3 hard-cooked eggs
½ cup slivered cooked ham
3 green onions and tops
¼ cup vinegar
1 teaspoon sugar
Salt
Worcestershire
Pepper
2 tablespoons chopped ripe olives

You would be right to call this either a chef's salad or a wilted lettuce salad—it borrows ideas from both.

Cook bacon until crisp; drain. Save 4 tablespoons bacon drippings in pan. Place greens in salad bowl. Chop eggs, arrange on greens with ham. Slice onions and sauté in drippings. Add vinegar and sugar. Add salt, Worcestershire, and pepper to taste. Pour hot dressing over greens, crumble bacon on top, sprinkle with the chopped ripe olives, and toss. Makes 6 servings.

Orange and Cucumber Green Salad

3 large oranges
1 small cucumber
2 heads butter lettuce
½ red onion

DRESSING:
½ cup salad oil
3 tablespoons wine vinegar
¼ teaspoon chili powder
Salt and freshly ground pepper
  to taste

Peel and slice oranges (remove all membrane), and slice cucumbers (peel if desired). Thinly slice onion and separate into rings. Arrange whole leaves of butter lettuce in a large, shallow salad bowl. Tuck orange slices and cucumber slices among the lettuce leaves. Arrange onion rings in overlapping circles on top of the salad.
  For the dressing, combine salad oil, vinegar, chili powder, salt, and freshly ground pepper. Sprinkle on salad just before serving. Makes 8 servings.

Greek Salad

¼ head of iceberg lettuce
¼ head of romaine
18 medium-sized radishes
¼ pound crumbled Feta cheese
1 small can (2 oz.) anchovy fillets,
minced
2 medium-sized tomatoes, cut in
small pieces
1 tablespoon chopped fresh parsley
¼ teaspoon dried oregano,
crumbled
Freshly ground pepper

DRESSING:
½ cup olive oil
2 tablespoons tarragon vinegar
½ teaspoon salt
¼ teaspoon freshly ground pepper
2 tablespoons mixed fresh herbs
(marjoram, rosemary, tarragon,
savory, chives, chervil or parsley)
2 bunches green onions and tops

Two hours before serving, tear the lettuce and romaine into a salad bowl. Add whole radishes, cheese, anchovies, tomatoes, parsley, oregano, and freshly ground pepper. Toss gently, cover with a damp tea towel, and chill.

For the dressing, shake together in a pint bottle oil, vinegar, salt, pepper, and herbs. When ready to serve, pour dressing over salad and toss. Poke green onions straight up in center of salad. Makes 6 to 8 servings.

FRUIT SALADS

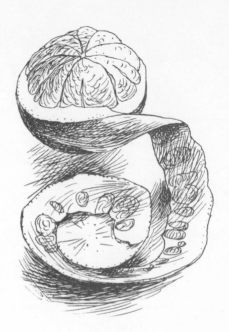

A Fruit Salad

fits gracefully into many menus; and for salad beauty, there is no lovelier choice. Combining fresh fruits in a salad is one of the best ways to show off their beautiful colors and shapes; and when fresh fruits are not in season, canned and frozen fruits are delicious and taste-tempting alternates.

A "fruit salad bar" is an eye-catching addition to a buffet table. Serve platters of assorted fruits attractively arranged in rows: thin slices of pineapple; halved, sliced, peeled oranges; grapes plucked from their stems, and seeded if necessary; sliced pears, bananas, and apples (dipped in lemon juice); avocados, papayas, grapefruit, and persimmons. Offer a choice of two or three dressings: French, sour cream, and a thin mayonnaise are good choices. Place chilled salad plates and a bowl of crisp greens nearby, and let guests make their own selections of fruits.

The dressing for a fruit salad may be tossed with the salad ingredients, as in Waldorf Salad, or it may be served in a separate bowl. When grapefruit or other juicy fruit is to be tossed with greens, it is a good idea to toss the lettuce with the dressing first and then arrange the fruit over the salad so that fruit retains its shape and the juices do not dilute the dressing.

Fresh Fruit Salad with Cranberry Dressing

⅓ cup mayonnaise
½ cup jellied cranberry sauce
Juice of ½ lemon
Juice of ½ small orange
¼ teaspoon dry mustard
2 teaspoons sugar
1 large fresh pineapple or 1 can
(1 lb., 4 oz.) sliced pineapple
Butter lettuce or other greens
3 bananas
2 or 3 soft ripe persimmons

Fresh fruits of the autumn season make a colorful salad plate, especially when you serve a bowl of this unusual cranberry dressing to top each salad. You might scatter pomegranate seeds over each salad for extra brightness.

For the dressing blend together mayonnaise, cranberry sauce, lemon juice, orange juice, mustard, and sugar. Chill. Peel pineapple and slice, removing core. On 6 to 8 individual salad plates covered with crisp greens, arrange a slice of pineapple. Peel and slice bananas into the center of the pineapple ring, and arrange sliced persimmon in spoke fashion on top. Pass the dressing separately for each diner to serve himself. Makes 6 to 8 servings.

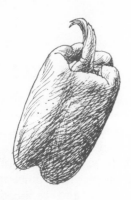

California Fruit Salad

Arrange, alternately, sections of peeled fresh grapefruit, avocado slices, and peeled orange sections on a bed of chicory, and sprinkle rather thickly with minced green and red bell peppers. Serve with French dressing.

Fruit Salad in Romaine Leaves

1 pint country-style cottage cheese
¼ teaspoon seasoned salt
3 tablespoons mayonnaise
½ cup coarsely chopped pecans,
cashews, or walnuts
1½ cups cut-up fruit or whole
berries (such as cantaloupe or
honeydew melon, fresh peaches,
grapes, strawberries)
6 medium-sized romaine leaves

MINT DRESSING:
½ cup mint jelly
¼ cup salad oil
¼ teaspoon grated lime peel
2 or 3 tablespoons lime juice
Salt

Combine cottage cheese, seasoned salt, and mayonnaise. Gently stir in nuts and fruit. Spoon some of the fruit and cheese mixture into each romaine leaf. Arrange filled leaves on a large platter. Serve with Mint Dressing. Makes 6 servings.

Beat mint jelly with a rotary beater until smooth. Add salad oil, lime peel, lime juice, and a few grains of salt. Stir until blended. Makes about ¾ cup dressing.

Fruit Salad with Pecan Dressing

½ cup salad oil
¼ cup orange juice
1 tablespoon lemon juice
1 teaspoon sugar
¼ teaspoon salt
¼ cup finely chopped,
  toasted pecan meats
1 cup cubed fresh or
  canned pineapple
2 bananas, sliced
1 cup Thompson seedless grapes
2 pears, peeled and diced
2 red-skinned apples, diced

This tart salad dressing has chopped nut meats mixed in it. Sliced papaya would make a good addition to the fresh fruit combination.

Pour salad oil and orange juice into a 1-pint screw top jar or plastic shaker. Add lemon juice, sugar, salt, and chopped nut meats. (If you toast pecan meats in a moderate oven (350°) for 10 minutes, they are more crisp and flavorful.) Cover tightly and shake until dressing is mixed thoroughly. Makes 1 cup dressing. Toss together chilled pineapple, sliced bananas, grapes, diced pears, and diced apples. Pour dressing over fruit and toss lightly. Makes 6 servings.

Mexican Salad

8 small cooked beets
4 peeled oranges
4 unpeeled, cored red apples
4 peeled bananas
Fruit from 1 fresh pineapple, or 1
can (1 lb., 14 oz.) pineapple chunks
3 limes, peeled
1 head lettuce
¼ cup sugar (optional)
Seeds of 2 ripe pomegranates
1 cup peanuts, chopped
1 cup tart French dressing (¾ cup
oil, ¼ cup red wine vinegar, salt)
or 1 cup orange juice

Slice or dice the beets and various fruits and shred the lettuce. Put lettuce in the bottom of a large shallow bowl and arrange fruits and all other ingredients in layers, sprinkling with the sugar, if you choose to use it. Have the top layer pictorially attractive, perhaps with a ring of oranges around the outer edge, then beets, then pineapple in the center, with pomegranate seeds and chopped peanuts sprinkled over all. Just before serving, pour on the French dressing or the orange juice (which the Mexicans sometimes prefer) and mix gently. Makes about 8 servings.

Waldorf Salad

6 firm, tart, red apples
2 tablespoons lemon juice
1½ cups sliced celery
½ cup coarsely chopped walnuts
Salad dressing or mayonnaise
  (about ¾ cup)
Lettuce

Wash apples, quarter, core, and dice coarsely without peeling; sprinkle with lemon juice and toss to prevent discoloration. Add celery, nuts, and salad dressing or mayonnaise to moisten well. Serve at once on lettuce. Makes 6 servings.

Creamy Waldorf Salad

1 package (3 oz.) cream cheese
¼ cup evaporated milk
2 teaspoons sugar
¾ teaspoon salt
Dash of pepper
2 tablespoons vinegar
2 cups diced, unpared apples
⅔ cup diced celery
¼ cup finely chopped nut meats
(optional)

A piquant cream cheese dressing is prepared in advance and chilled for this interesting variation of the classic Waldorf salad. Apples, celery, and nut meats are added just before serving.

Put cream cheese into a bowl; gradually stir in evaporated milk, mixing until smooth. Add sugar, salt, pepper, and vinegar; beat until smooth and fluffy. Chill. Just before time to serve, add apples, celery, and nut meats. Toss lightly with a fork. Serve on lettuce. Makes 4 servings.

Apple and Cauliflower Salad

4 cups thinly sliced
unpeeled Delicious apples
1 cup thin slices raw cauliflower
Mayonnaise (about ¾ cup)
Salt
Pepper
Lettuce cups

Cut apple slices in thirds, crosswise. Toss with cauliflower and enough mayonnaise to coat each piece. Season to taste with salt and pepper. (Add a little lemon juice if you like a more tart salad.) Chill thoroughly and serve from lettuce cups. Makes 5 to 6 servings.

Fall Fruit and Nut Tray

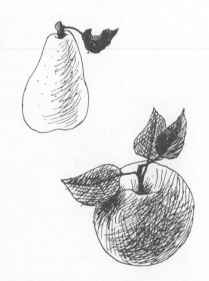

From fruits in season—such as apples, pears, figs, pineapple, persimmons, bananas, grapes, quinces, guavas—select an assortment of your favorites. Allow 1 or 2 whole fruits, or about 1 cup fruit for each serving. Prepare fruit to eat—peel, pare, seed, and core as is necessary. Cut fruit in about two-bite-size portions (but cut grapes in halves) and arrange each fruit individually in a row on a large tray. Garnish with salted nuts if you wish or serve the nuts in a separate bowl. Let each person select the combination for his own salad. Spoon dressing over each serving.

CHEESE AND NUT DRESSING:
Whip until smooth 1 package (8 oz.) cream cheese with ¼ cup milk and 2 tablespoons lemon juice. Blend ½ cup finely chopped salted macadamia nuts or cashews (or both), 1 cup grated sharp Cheddar cheese, 2 tablespoons sugar, ¼ teaspoon pepper, and salt to taste. Add more milk if you prefer a thinner dressing. Makes about 3 cups.

Cheese and Apple Salad

1 cup chopped red-skinned apple
1 cup sliced celery
½ cup diced Cheddar cheese, cut in ½-inch cubes
½ cup diced pineapple, fresh or canned
4 tablespoons (¼ cup) mayonnaise
3 tablespoons lemon juice
1 teaspoon sugar
¼ teaspoon salt
Lettuce cups

Combine the apple, celery, cheese, and pineapple. Stir together until smooth the mayonnaise, lemon juice, sugar, and salt; pour over apple mixture and stir until well coated; chill. To serve, spoon into crisp lettuce cups. Makes 4 to 6 servings.

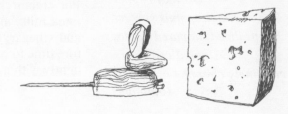

Bacon and Apple Salad

1 cup crumbled fried bacon
½ cup diced apple
½ cup sliced celery
4 tablespoons (¼ cup) mayonnaise

Combine crumbled bacon, apple, celery, and mayonnaise. You may wish to add some lemon or orange juice if the apples are not very tart and juicy. Serve in lettuce cups. Makes 3 or 4 servings.

Avocado Halves with Citrus Dressing

½ cup powdered sugar
1 tablespoon paprika
1¼ teaspoons salt
1 clove garlic, peeled and cut in half
1 tablespoon Worcestershire
1 cup salad oil
3 tablespoons lemon juice
¼ cup tarragon vinegar
½ cup orange juice
4 medium-sized avocados
Endive

Because it contains a large amount of acid, this orange-colored dressing keeps avocado on the half shell from darkening.

Put the sugar, paprika, salt, garlic, and Worcestershire in a 1-quart jar. Pour in the oil, lemon juice, vinegar, and orange juice; cover and shake until well blended. Let stand several hours for flavors to blend. Remove garlic and shake again before using. Cut avocados in half lengthwise, remove seeds (do not peel), and arrange on endive. Spoon dressing into cavities and over fruit. Makes 8 servings (dressing makes 2 cups).

Avocado-Popcorn Salad

For a real conversation piece, place half of an unpeeled avocado on a bed of lettuce. Then fill the cavity with hot buttered popped corn. Sprinkle with rum or lemon juice. Serve at once.

Grapes in Avocado Half Shells

3 medium-sized avocados
1 tablespoon lemon juice
Salt
1 pound Red Malaga
or other red grapes
½ cup sliced celery (use white inner stalks)
¼ cup lime juice
¼ cup unsweetened pineapple juice
½ cup red table wine
2 teaspoons sugar
½ teaspoon brine from pickled hot peppers
Endive or chicory
Mint

This fruit platter, with its striking color combination of ruby, white, and avocado green, is ideal for a buffet.

Cut avocados in half lengthwise and remove seeds; brush with lemon juice and sprinkle lightly with salt. Cut grapes in half, remove seeds, and combine with the sliced celery; spoon mixture into the avocado centers.

Mix together lime juice, pineapple juice, wine, sugar, and pepper brine; pour over the stuffed avocados. Chill. Serve on a bed of endive or chicory, and garnish with mint. Makes 6 servings.

Avocado, Pear, and Pineapple Salad

Peel 4 avocados and peel and core 4 pears (choose ones of about equal size). Slice, dice, or cut fruit in crescents. Arrange in a ring or pinwheel fashion on a bed of romaine and iceberg lettuce with 1 cup finely chopped fresh, frozen, or canned pineapple in the center. Sprinkle with lemon juice. Pour a plain French dressing over salad and serve. Makes 8 to 10 servings.

Baked Avocado Halves

2 firm, medium-sized avocados
1 egg white
⅓ cup mayonnaise
Pinch of salt
4 lettuce cups

The dressing bakes right into this avocado to offset the richness. Garnish with slivers of cooked chicken breast for a main dish.

Peel avocados, cut in half, remove seeds, and place in a lightly greased baking pan. Beat egg white until stiff, then fold in mayonnaise and salt. Pile mixture lightly into avocado cavities. Bake in a moderate oven (350°) for 8 minutes. Slip pan under broiler for several minutes or until meringue is lightly browned. Place in lettuce cups and serve immediately. Makes 4 servings.

Curried Avocado Rings

1 large avocado
Lemon juice
1 small package (3 oz.) cream cheese
2 tablespoons crumbled blue cheese
3 tablespoons each chopped ripe olives and nut meats
1 tablespoon chopped chives
Grated peel and juice of 1 lime
2 teaspoons evaporated milk or light cream
¾ teaspoon curry powder
¼ teaspoon salt
Dash of cayenne
Crisp greens
Grapefruit sections
French dressing

Because these avocado rings are so attractive, they are ideal to serve at a luncheon party. The rich curry-seasoned filling is especially appealing.

Cut avocado in half, remove seed, and peel. Enlarge the cavity in each half by scooping out some of the avocado. (This may be mashed and combined with cream cheese for a sandwich filling.) Brush avocado halves with lemon juice. Combine cream cheese, blue cheese, olives, nut meats, chives, grated lime peel and juice, milk, curry powder, salt, and cayenne. Pack cheese mixture into avocado halves, press halves together; wrap in foil; chill. To serve, cut stuffed avocado crosswise into 6 slices. Place each round on crisp greens, garnish with grapefruit sections, and serve with a tart French dressing. Makes 6 servings.

Avocado Half Shells with Caviar

For each serving arrange half an unpeeled avocado on a bed of butter lettuce on individual salad plates. Spoon 1 tablespoon domestic caviar into the center of each avocado half shell, and garnish lightly with finely chopped white onion. Pour over plain French dressing.

Avocado Halves with Hot Cocktail Sauce

4 tablespoons (¼ cup) butter or margarine
4 tablespoons (¼ cup) catsup
2 tablespoons vinegar
2 tablespoons water
1 tablespoon sugar
2 teaspoons Worcestershire
⅓ teaspoon salt
Dash of Tabasco
3 small avocados

For an easy-to-make appetizer, fill avocado half shells with this heated, spicy sauce which will contrast with the cool, butter-smooth avocado.

In the top of a double boiler, mix together the butter, catsup, vinegar, water, sugar, Worcestershire, salt, and Tabasco to taste. Heat over boiling water until butter has melted and sauce is smooth. Cut avocados in half lengthwise, separate halves, and remove seeds. Spoon hot sauce into avocados and serve as an appetizer. Makes 6 servings.

Avocado Half Shells with Mandarin Oranges

Cut 1 medium-sized avocado in half, remove seed, and sprinkle cut sides with lemon juice. Arrange on salad plates on a bed of endive. Spoon canned mandarin orange sections into each avocado cavity and pour French dressing over avocado and endive. Makes 2 servings.

Grapefruit-Avocado Salad

1 large grapefruit (pink or white)
2 medium-sized avocados
1 head curly endive
1 pimiento
1 cup tart French dressing

A sharp contrast in flavor and texture—fresh tangy grapefruit, buttery ripe avocado. The slightly bitter flavor and the feathery curls of endive make an ideal background for grapefruit and avocado.

Cut grapefruit into segments and remove membrane. Peel avocado; cut in slices about ¾ inch wide, or the width of the grapefruit segments. Break endive into small pieces and arrange on 4 salad plates, with the lighter colored leaves in the center. On each bed of endive, alternate 4 avocado slices and 3 grapefruit sections, arranging them to form a compact half circle. Cut pimiento along one of its folded sides into four 1-inch strips about ⅛ inch wide, and arrange in a V over the pointed end of the avocado slices. Shake the French dressing well and pour over. Makes 4 servings.

Cottage Cheese-Banana Salad

4 ripe bananas
Head lettuce and romaine
1 pint cottage cheese
1 cup whole cranberry sauce
Chopped salted almonds (optional)

Cranberry sauce makes a sweet-tart dressing for this cottage cheese salad. Canned or fresh pear halves can be used in place of the bananas.

Peel bananas, cut in half lengthwise, then arrange on lettuce and romaine leaves. Spread a layer of cottage cheese over the top of each banana half, then top with a spoonful of cranberry sauce. Sprinkle with chopped nuts if desired. Makes 8 servings.

Curried Banana Salad

3 medium-sized bananas
1 tablespoon lemon juice
¾ cup cooked rice, chilled
¼ cup sliced celery
½ cup seedless grapes
¼ cup finely chopped salted
peanuts
1 tablespoon minced chives
2 tablespoons canned pimientos,
cut in fine strips
Few drops Tabasco

DRESSING:
½ cup mayonnaise
2 tablespoons light cream
1 tablespoon lemon juice or
lime juice
1 teaspoon curry powder
½ teaspoon dry mustard
Chicory or other crisp greens
1 tablespoon toasted coconut
2 tablespoons chopped chutney

You can make this curry-flavored fruit salad ahead. It's a fine accompaniment for chicken, lamb, fish, or shellfish.

Cut the bananas in ½-inch slices; sprinkle immediately with the lemon juice. Add rice, celery, grapes, peanuts, chives, pimiento, and Tabasco, toss lightly. Chill.

Combine the mayonnaise with cream, lemon juice, curry, and mustard. To serve add dressing to the salad, toss lightly with 2 forks. Arrange on chilled greens; sprinkle with coconut and top with a small mound chutney. Makes 4 to 6 servings.

Citrus Lettuce Salad

1 head lettuce
½ bunch water cress
1 grapefruit, sectioned
2 medium-sized oranges, sectioned
12 dates, pitted
¼ cup chopped preserved ginger
1 package (3 oz.) cream cheese

Some unusual ingredients, including orange and grapefruit sections, dates, and water cress, make this tossed lettuce salad outstanding.

Break lettuce and water cress into bite-size pieces in a salad bowl. Add grapefruit and orange sections, dates, and ginger. Add just enough Citrus Dressing to moisten slightly. Crumble cream cheese into salad and toss lightly. Makes about 5 servings.

CITRUS DRESSING:
Combine in a covered jar ½ cup sugar, ⅓ cup *each* vinegar and catsup, 1 teaspoon salt, 1 small finely chopped onion, and 1 clove garlic (minced or mashed). Add enough salad oil (about 1 cup) to make 1 pint of dressing. Cover, shake well, and chill. Makes about 2 cups of dressing.

Cherry Fruit Salad

1 head of iceberg lettuce
or 2 heads of butter lettuce
1 medium-sized cataloupe, peeled
and cut in cubes
1 small pineapple, peeled and cut in
chunks or 1 can (1 lb. 13 oz.)
pineapple chunks, drained
1 avocado, peeled and diced
1½ cups pitted Bing
or Royal Ann cherries
½ teaspoon salt
Juice of ½ lemon

DRESSING:
2 tablespoons sesame seeds
1 cup (½ pint) commercial sour
cream
Juice of 1 lime
3 tablespoons undiluted frozen
orange juice concentrate
¼ teaspoon salt

Line a salad bowl with lettuce cups and tear the remaining greens into bite-size chunks. Lightly toss together the lettuce chunks with the cantaloupe, pineapple, avocado, cherries, salt, and lemon juice. Pile in the salad bowl; chill.

For the dressing, sprinkle the sesame seeds in a shallow pan and toast in a moderate oven (350°) for 10 minutes, or until golden brown. Mix together the sour cream, lime juice, orange juice concentrate, salt, and toasted sesame seeds. Serve in a separate dish to accompany the salad. Makes 6 servings.

Fruit and Vegetable Salad

1 large can (1 lb. 14 oz.) fruit
cocktail mix
1 medium can (11 oz.) mandarin
orange sections
1½ cups slivered raw carrots
½ head lettuce, finely chopped
Pinch of salt
Mayonnaise and lemon juice to taste

Drain the juice from the fruit cocktail mix and the mandarin oranges. Combine fruit with the carrots and the lettuce. Toss with salt and enough mayonnaise to moisten. Taste, then add lemon juice to give mixture sufficient tartness. Makes 6 servings.

Minted Citrus Salad

On a bed of salad greens (leaf lettuce, butter lettuce, or romaine tips) arrange 2 cups fresh grapefruit sections and 2 or 3 large oranges, peeled and thinly sliced. Garnish with mint leaves. Ladle some of this dressing on each serving: Blend together 3 tablespoons mint jelly, 1 tablespoon honey, grated peel and juice of 1 lime, and juice of 1 lemon. Makes 6 servings.

Orange Salad

1 medium-sized head of lettuce

2 medium-sized tomatoes, peeled and thinly sliced

Salt and freshly ground pepper

1 small onion, very thinly sliced crosswise

1 or 2 teaspoons vinegar

2 large oranges, peeled (remove white membrane) and sliced crosswise

2 teaspoons sugar

Canned or cooked beet slices cut in star shapes

Radish flowers

The intriguing blend of oranges, onion slices, and tomatoes with vinegar and sugar—and no other dressing—makes this salad an especially good choice for those who are counting calories.

Arrange outer leaves of lettuce in bottom of a salad bowl; save the heart to use as garnish. Lay tomato slices on lettuce; salt and pepper. Distribute onion slices over tomatoes; salt, pepper, and sprinkle with vinegar. Arrange orange slices on onions, and sprinkle with sugar. Refrigerate for 15 minutes; garnish with lettuce heart, beet stars, and radish flowers. Makes 6 servings.

Orange and Beet Salad Plate

Citrus fruits so often give the sharp tang we desire in a salad. Try this teaming of fresh orange slices and sliced beet rounds for a colorful citrus salad.

Alternate slices of orange and beets on a bed of endive or water cress and serve with this dressing: Mix together 6 tablespoons salad oil, 2 tablespoons vinegar, ¼ teaspoon prepared mustard, 1 teaspoon finely chopped parsley, and ½ teaspoon *each* dried chervil and tarragon. Makes ½ cup dressing.

Crunchy Fruit Salad

1 can (3 oz.) crisp Chinese noodles

3 medium-sized oranges

¾ cup canned or fresh grapefruit segments

1 cup pineapple chunks

¼ cup French dressing

Toasted sesame seeds

Crisp Chinese noodles replace lettuce in this fruit salad. It is an especially good accompaniment to roast pork or spareribs. To toast sesame seeds, place in a heavy frying pan; stirring, cook over medium heat until browned, about 5 minutes.

Arrange beds of noodles on 5 individual salad plates. Peel oranges and cut in ¼-inch-thick slices. Arrange sliced oranges, well-drained grapefruit segments, and pineapple chunks on noodles. Just before serving, pour French dressing over each salad, then sprinkle generously with toasted sesame seeds. Makes 5 servings.

Orange, Onion, and Olive Salad

3 medium-sized oranges
1 Bermuda onion
1 dozen pitted ripe olives, sliced
¼ pound Roquefort cheese
1 clove garlic, minced or mashed
½ cup French dressing
Lettuce

The Roquefort cheese dressing gives orange and onion salad a new flavor emphasis. Grapefruit segments from which all the white membrane has been removed may be added just before serving.

Peel oranges and cut in crosswise slices. Peel onion and cut in very thin slices. Toss onion and oranges together in a bowl with the sliced ripe olives. Mash the Roquefort cheese in a bowl, stir in the garlic, then moisten with the French dressing. Pour over the oranges and onion and let marinate for 1 hour. Serve in crisp lettuce cups. Makes 6 servings.

Citrus Salad

2 tablespoons honey
2 tablespoons tarragon vinegar
1 teaspoon ground cardamom
5 or 6 dashes of Angostura bitters
½ teaspoon onion salt
2 fresh grapefruit
3 large oranges

You won't notice that oil is missing from the dressing on this salad. All other ingredients combine to cut down the sharpness of the citrus fruits. Canned, unsweetened grapefruit segments may be used as a substitute for the fresh.

Mix together honey, vinegar, cardamom, bitters, and onion salt. Cut grapefruit into segments; slice oranges. Toss together with dressing. Serve as a bowl salad, with or without lettuce. Makes 6 servings.

Grapefruit Pinwheels with Cheese-Stuffed Prunes

2 small packages (3 oz. each)
cream cheese
3 tablespoons mayonnaise
Dash of salt
¼ cup finely chopped pecan meats
16 large pitted, cooked
dried prunes
4 large grapefruit
1 bunch endive

No dressing is needed for this combination of grapefruit sections and spicy sweet prunes, plumped with cheese and pecans.

Cream together the cheese (warmed to room temperature), mayonnaise, and salt; mix in the nut meats. Stuff some of the cheese mixture into each prune. Peel and section grapefruit. For each serving arrange 6 or 7 fresh grapefruit sections in the shape of a pinwheel on a bed of endive on salad plates. Center 2 stuffed prunes in each pinwheel. Makes 8 servings.

Cranberry Grape Salad

1 pound (4 cups) cranberries
1⅔ cups sugar
2 cups Tokay grapes, halved
and seeded
1 cup sliced celery
1 cup chopped nut meats
12 marshmallows, quartered
½ pint (1 cup) whipping cream
Lettuce

You sugar the ground raw cranberries to draw out their scarlet juice, which literally dyes this salad a rosy red. The juicy Tokays lend a crackling bite. This fruit combination is sweet enough for dessert.

Grind cranberries through the fine blade of the food chopper into a medium-sized bowl; add sugar and let stand while you assemble the other ingredients. Add the grapes, celery, nut meats, and marshmallows to the cranberries. Whip cream and fold in thoroughly. Chill for several hours. Serve in lettuce cups. Makes 12 servings.

Grape Jumble Salad

Segments from ½ medium-sized
grapefruit
1 cup seedless grapes
1 fresh pear, peeled, cored,
and diced
1 can (11 oz.) mandarin oranges,
drained
4 tablespoons (¼ cup) olive oil
or salad oil
1 tablespoon each lemon
and lime juice
1 teaspoon salt
¼ teaspoon paprika
Few grains cayenne
Chicory and water cress

Place grapefruit segments in a bowl with grapes, diced pear, and oranges. Combine olive oil, lemon juice, lime juice, salt, paprika, and cayenne; pour over fruit, and toss together lightly. Chill in refrigerator. Serve on crisp greens. Makes 6 servings.

Tomato and Cantaloupe Ball Salad

1 cantaloupe
2 tomatoes
½ cup French dressing
Salt and pepper to taste
2 sprigs mint (optional)
Endive

Cantaloupe half shells serve as the bowls for this simple, good-looking salad.

Cut cantaloupe in half, remove seeds, and scoop the pulp into balls. Cut the stem end from the tomatoes and cut into wedges. Mix together the cantaloupe balls and tomato wedges and refill each half shell. Pour over French dressing, and sprinkle with salt and pepper to taste; garnish with mint. Serve on a bed of endive. Garnish each salad with a wedge of lime for added tang. Makes 2 servings.

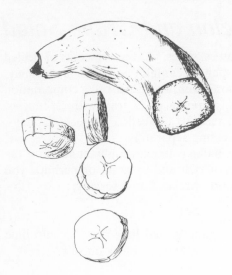

Fruit Salad Plate

Toss together a mixture of cantaloupe cubes, slightly crushed and sweetened raspberries, and banana slices. Heap on a plate lined with salad greens and garnish with lime wedges.

Cantaloupe and Cherry Salad

Peel 1 ripe cantaloupe, cut into slices about 1 inch wide, and remove seeds. Put each melon ring on a bed of lettuce and fill the center with pitted dark, sweet cherries. Serve with French dressing. Makes 6 to 8 servings.

Cantaloupe and Onion Salad

3 cups cantaloupe balls
2 small onions
1 medium-sized head lettuce
¾ cup tart French dressing

Pair cantaloupe balls with onions that are mild and sweet in flavor.

Chill cantaloupe balls; cut onions in half and thinly slice; shred lettuce. Mix chilled melon balls with onions and lettuce. Pour over French dressing and toss. Makes 10 servings.

Tropical Salad

1 small papaya
2 slices (1 inch thick) fresh pineapple
or 1 cup frozen pineapple pieces
2 mangoes or 1 can (14 oz.) mangoes
2 medium-sized oranges

AVOCADO DRESSING:
1 large ripe avocado
½ cup orange juice
1½ teaspoons lemon juice
2 teaspoons sugar
¼ teaspoon salt
Water cress

Here's a recipe for a salad which calls for fruits of both subtropical and tropical origin. The avocado dressing, with its bright green color, is the ideal foil for the yellow and orange-colored fruits.

Cut papaya in half, scrape out seeds, peel, and dice. Cut fresh pineapple slices in pieces or use the frozen. Peel mangoes, remove seed, and cut fruit into small pieces or slices. Peel oranges, removing all membrane; slice, then cut into pieces. Combine all fruits and chill.

Cut avocado in half, remove seed, peel and mash. Add orange juice, lemon juice, sugar, and salt gradually; beat thoroughly. Chill.

Arrange chilled fruits on bed of water cress and serve with the avocado dressing. Makes 6 to 8 servings.

Melon and Grape Salad

Prepare 4 cups of cubes, slices, or slim crescents of peeled and seeded melon such as cantaloupe, crenshaw, honeydew, or casaba; choose your favorite or use a combination of several varieties. Arrange on a tray with 2 cups of grapes—Thompson seedless or seeded Muscats, Tokays, or Ribiers. Serve dressing separately.

Serve the first if you like your dressing light and tart, the second if you prefer it rich and creamy; or perhaps you would like to offer both. Makes 4 to 6 servings.

LIGHT LIME DRESSING:
Shake together 1 teaspoon grated lime peel, ⅓ cup lime juice, 1 tablespoon honey, and ¼ teaspoon salt.

CREAMY LIME DRESSING:
Blend together ¾ cup commercial sour cream, 3 tablespoons limeade concentrate, ½ teaspoon *each* grated lemon and orange peel, ½ teaspoon minced preserved ginger, and 1 tablespoon sugar.

Papaya Salad

1 ripe papaya, approximately
1½ pounds
1½ cups diced pineapple
1¼ cups sliced celery
¼ cup finely chopped onion
¼ cup sliced ripe olives
¼ teaspoon salt
¾ cup mayonnaise
Lettuce cups

Cut the papaya in half lengthwise and remove seeds. Remove pulp, dice it, and place in a mixing bowl. Combine with pineapple, celery, onion, olives, salt, and mayonnaise. Chill. Serve in lettuce cups. Makes 6 servings.

Papaya, Orange, Avocado

Peel 1 papaya; cut in halves or quarters and remove seeds. Peel 3 medium-sized oranges, cutting away white membrane; slice thinly crosswise, removing as many seeds as possible. Peel, cut in halves, and pit 2 ripe avocados. Let fruit marinate several hours in chili dressing in refrigerator; drain and arrange on tray. Offer dressing with each serving. Makes 4 servings.

CHILI DRESSING:
Combine ¼ cup *each* salad oil and lemon juice, 1 tablespoon finely minced dry or green onion, ½ teaspoon chili powder, ½ teaspoon salt, and ¼ teaspoon freshly ground black pepper.

Papaya Star Salad

2 papayas
1 cup pineapple-cottage cheese
1 small package (3 oz.) cream cheese
¼ teaspoon salt
2 tablespoons lemon juice
Lettuce
French dressing

Cheese complements the delicate flavor of papaya in this salad. It is attractive in appearance, too.

Cut tops from papayas about a quarter of the way down. Scoop out seeds with a teaspoon—carefully so as not to spoil the star outline in the center. Combine cottage and cream cheeses, salt, and lemon juice, and mix until smooth. Spoon into papayas, packing down as much as possible. Chill 1 to 2 hours. Cut crosswise in 1½-inch slices, and serve on lettuce or leaf-garnished salad plates with a simple French dressing or a sprinkling of lemon or lime. Makes 4 to 6 servings.

Fruit-Filled Watermelon Shell with Tart Sauce

1 large, ripe watermelon
Selection of fresh fruits (combine any or all of the following with bite-size pieces or balls cut from the watermelon heart; for a large melon shell, you will need 3 to 4 quarts bite-size fruits and about 1 quart melon pieces):
Pitted sweet cherries
Ripe melon (other than watermelon), cut into balls or bite-size pieces
Strawberries
Raspberries
Fresh pineapple, cut into chunks
Peaches, sliced
Pears, sliced or diced
Seeded grapes

Take time to select the right watermelon to make the "boat" for this lavish, fresh fruit salad. It should be a large, ripe, oval-shaped melon that rests securely on one side.

Place washed melon on flat side and cut a large window in the top, removing about ⅓ of the shell. Take out melon heart, leaving a layer of pink to form a bed for the salad. Cut the heart of the melon into balls or bite-size pieces for the fruit salad mixture. Cut a sawtooth edge on melon shell with a sharp knife. Turn upside down and allow to drain thoroughly; chill. At serving time, fill shell with combined fresh fruit. Offer Tart Sauce (below). Makes 12 to 15 servings.

TART SAUCE:
⅔ cup fresh orange juice
¼ cup fresh lemon juice
½ cup sugar
Dash salt
4 egg yolks, slightly beaten
1½ cups heavy cream, whipped
Grated orange peel

Combine in top of double boiler the orange and lemon juice, sugar, and salt. Cook over direct heat until syrup simmers. Place over hot water and gradually add egg yolks, beating constantly. Continue to cook and stir over hot (not boiling) water until smooth and thick. Chill. Fold in whipped cream. Turn into serving bowl; sprinkle with orange peel.

Peach-Cheese Salad

1½ cups cottage cheese
¼ cup mayonnaise
1 cup diced peaches
¼ cup slivered salted almonds
Few grains salt
Shredded lettuce
Peach slices
French dressing

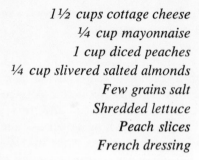

You'll find this salad light but filling enough for mid-day meals. The crisp saltiness of the almonds adds interest.

Gently combine all ingredients. Pile attractively on shredded lettuce. Garnish with peach slices and serve with a creamy French dressing. Makes 4 servings.

Cheese-Stuffed Pear Salad

¼ cup (4 tablespoons) port or other red dessert wine
1 teaspoon cornstarch
¼ cup (4 tablespoons) currant jelly
½ cup mayonnaise
2 teaspoons lemon juice
2 teaspoons grated lemon peel
⅛ teaspoon salt
½ cup whipping cream
Red food coloring
1 large can (1 lb. 13 oz.) pear halves
¼ cup crumbled blue
or Roquefort cheese
¼ cup grated Cheddar cheese
Salad greens

The currant jelly and wine dressing pick up the mild flavor of pears. Fresh winter pear halves, brushed with lemon juice, can substitute for canned pears.

To make dressing, combine wine and cornstarch in a saucepan and stir until blended. Add currant jelly. Stirring constantly, cook until mixture boils. Cool. Stir in mayonnaise, lemon juice and peel, and salt. Whip cream until stiff and fold in. Add enough red food coloring to tint dressing a pale rose color. Chill.

Drain pear halves. Blend blue and Cheddar cheeses with a fork. Stuff the cavities of 4 pear halves with cheese mixture, and put another pear half on top of each; poke 2 toothpicks into pear halves to hold in place. Arrange on greens and top with dressing. Makes 4 servings.

Pear-Mango Salad

1 small fresh pineapple
1 cup creamed cottage cheese
2 pears, peeled and cut in chunks
1 mango, peeled and sliced
1½ tablespoons sliced preserved ginger
1½ tablespoons toasted, sliced Brazil nut meats
Sweet French dressing

Heaped in the pineapple half shells, this attractive fresh fruit and cottage cheese salad tastes as good as it looks.

Beginning at the crown, cut pineapple in half lengthwise; scoop out the fruit, using a grapefruit knife. In the bottom of each half, place a layer of cottage cheese. Remove core from pineapple and cut fruit into chunks; place a layer over the cottage cheese. Arrange a layer each of pears and mangoes over the pineapple. Top with a sprinkling of ginger and nut meats, and serve with a sweet French dressing. Makes 2 servings as luncheon entrée, or 4 to 6 as side salad.

Pears with Filbert Cheese Balls

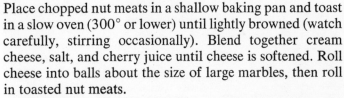

⅔ cup very finely chopped filberts
1 large package (8 oz.) cream cheese
Pinch of salt
3 tablespoons maraschino cherry juice
8 winter pears or 2 cans (1 lb. 13 oz. each) pear halves
Romaine or other crisp greens

Cream cheese balls, tinted with maraschino cherry juice and rolled in chopped roasted filberts, adorn a platter of juicy winter pears or canned pears.

Place chopped nut meats in a shallow baking pan and toast in a slow oven (300° or lower) until lightly browned (watch carefully, stirring occasionally). Blend together cream cheese, salt, and cherry juice until cheese is softened. Roll cheese into balls about the size of large marbles, then roll in toasted nut meats.

Arrange pear halves, cut side up, on crisp greens on a large chop plate. (If using fresh pears, dip peeled and cored halves in lemon, orange, or pineapple juice to prevent discoloring.) Place two or three cheese balls in the hollow of each pear half. Serve with or without French dressing. Makes 8 servings with 2 halves apiece.

Stuffed Pear Salad

18 gingersnaps, crushed
½ cup drained crushed pineapple
1 large package (8 oz.) cream cheese
2 tablespoons mayonnaise
4 fresh winter pears or 8 canned pear halves
½ cup sugar
3 tablespoons lemon juice
½ cup orange juice
1 egg
¼ teaspoon salt
½ cup whipping cream
Lettuce or water cress

You may stuff either fresh winter pears or canned Bartletts with this gingersnap and cream cheese filling. The lemon dressing will hold up for several days in your refrigerator, but do not add whipped cream until just before serving.

Mix together the crushed gingersnaps, pineapple, cheese, and mayonnaise. Stuff halves of fresh or canned pears with the mixture and chill.

In a double boiler, mix sugar, lemon and orange juice, well-beaten egg, and salt. Cook over hot water until thickened, stirring constantly. When cool, mix with whipped cream. Use as the dressing over the stuffed pears, which have been arranged on crisp lettuce leaves or on sprigs of water cress.

Persimmon Compote

Combine equal portions of sliced ripe persimmons, melon balls, and fresh pineapple cubes. Sprinkle with fresh lime juice and serve chilled from pineapple shells, as a first course salad or a dessert.

Persimmon Fruit Salad

2 large, ripe persimmons
1 avocado
16 grapefruit sections
Shredded lettuce
French dressing

This color combination of orange, green, and light yellow makes a most attractive first-course salad.

Peel persimmons and cut into eighths. Peel avocado, cut into eighths, then cut each in half so that avocado pieces will be the same length as persimmon and grapefruit sections. Arrange fruit alternately on bed of shredded lettuce. Serve with French dressing. Makes 4 servings.

Persimmons with Horse-Radish Cream Dressing

3 large ripe persimmons, chilled
6 lettuce cups
½ cup whipping cream
1 tablespoon prepared horse-radish
¼ teaspoon salt
Paprika

Cut persimmons in half lengthwise; place each half in a lettuce cup on a salad plate. Whip cream stiff, and fold in horse-radish and salt. Spoon a generous dollop in the center of each persimmon half; dust with paprika. Serve with both spoon and fork. Makes 6 servings.

Pineapple Salad with Tomato and Avocado

2 cups fresh pineapple chunks
1 cup thinly sliced, peeled tomatoes
(or cherry tomatoes, cut in half)
1 cup diced avocado
4 tablespoons wine vinegar
2 tablespoons salad oil
Salt and freshly ground
pepper to taste
Salad greens

Combine pineapple chunks, tomatoes, and avocado.

For dressing, beat or shake together the wine vinegar, salad oil, salt, and pepper. Pour over salad and toss lightly. Chill for about 30 minutes. Serve on crisp salad greens (or in the pineapple shell basket described opposite). Makes about 6 servings.

Stuffed Fresh Pineapple Salad

1 medium-sized fresh pineapple
½ pint small curd
cottage cheese
(with chives, if desired)
1 stalk celery, finely chopped
1 small avocado
Juice of ½ lemon
4 green or red maraschino cherries
Greens

With a sharp knife, cut the pineapple in quarters lengthwise, leaving its share of the crown on each piece. Use a grapefruit knife to scoop out the fruit, leaving the shell and foliage intact. Cut off the core and dice the pineapple into a bowl. Mix in the cottage cheese and celery. Fill the shells with the salad mixture. Peel avocado and slice thinly; arrange 3 or 4 slices over each salad and sprinkle with lemon juice. Top with a cherry. Makes 4 servings.

Ideas for Cutting and Serving Fresh Pineapple

BASKET
STYLE

ZIG-ZAG
STYLE

FAMILY
STYLE

When you serve fresh pineapple, you can make it a feast for the eyes as well as the palate by cutting it to take advantage of the natural beauty of the fruit.

If cutting a fresh pineapple is new to you, bear in mind that the core of the fruit is quite fibrous and is usually cut away; also, you must make your cut far enough inside the shell to remove the eyes. The edible portion that remains will be about half of the whole fruit. The diagrams show basic cutting techniques. Have ready a large heavy knife and also a smaller thin-bladed knife. For cutting neatly along curved edges, you'll need a grapefruit knife.

BASKET STYLE
A dramatic way in which to use a large pineapple shell as a serving container for its own fruit is to cut it basket-style. For the simplest version, cut away peel and core from the fruit you remove in cutting the basket; cut fruit into bite-sized chunks and pile back into shell. The pineapple may be combined with other fruits if desired.

ZIG-ZAG STYLE
One of the simplest and most impressive ways to present an individual serving of fresh pineapple is what we call zig-zag pineapple. To make 4 servings, cut a medium-sized pineapple as shown in the sketch, left. Serve as is, or set a contrasting fruit in the openings formed by the zig-zag pieces of pineapple. Use any fresh fruit or berries in season: strawberries, papaya pieces, watermelon balls, sweet cherries, raspberries.

LUAU STYLE
The style of cutting pineapple illustrated on the following page is commonly identified with the Hawaiian feast known as the luau. Pre-cut pineapples with tops set back in place become part of a lavish fruit and flower centerpiece. At a luau the pineapple spears are usually eaten with the fingers.

FAMILY STYLE
Sometimes you'll prefer simply to prepare the fresh pineapple for eating, without serving it in its shell. The drawings at left show the easiest method of removing the peel, saving as much edible fruit as possible (if you wish, you can use the plume as a garnish on a serving tray). Cut the whole fruit into either slices or spears. Slices or spears can be cut in smaller pieces, if desired.

Pineapple Salad with Orange Cottage Cheese

LUAU
STYLE

An attractive buffet salad plate can be made with an adaptation of the luau-style of pineapple cutting. Follow first and second steps shown in the sketch above. Then, instead of cutting the whole fruit section into spears, cut crosswise into 4 to 6 thick slices. Cut the hollow pineapple shell crosswise to form a bowl that will hold about 2 cups of Creamy Dressing (recipe follows); set shell filled with dressing in the center of a large serving plate or tray. Using a small biscuit cutter, cut out the core of each pineapple slice and arrange slices on lettuce leaves in a circle around the pineapple shell bowl. Top each slice with a scoop of Orange Cottage Cheese (recipe follows). Each guest serves himself a cheese-topped pineapple slice, tops it with dressing. A large pineapple serves 4 to 6; to serve more, you can cut extra slices from a second pineapple. The dressing and cottage cheese recipes below serve about 8.

CREAMY DRESSING:
Whip 1 cup heavy cream with 1 teaspoon dry mustard and ⅛ teaspoon salt. Fold in ½ cup mayonnaise with 1 tablespoon *each* lemon juice and grenadine syrup or maraschino cherry juice, and 2 tablespoons *each* chopped maraschino cherries and toasted almonds. Makes 2 cups.

ORANGE COTTAGE CHEESE:
Blend 1 pint (2 cups) small curd cottage cheese with 1 teaspoon grated orange peel, and ¼ cup toasted chopped or slivered almonds.

Pineapple Salad with Roquefort Dressing

¼ cup crumbled Roquefort cheese
1 cup commercial sour cream
¼ cup mayonnaise
Dash of salt
2 to 3 tablespoons light cream
Fruit from 1 large fresh pineapple,
cut in quarter slices or finger shapes
¾ pound cooked, shelled shrimp
(if large, cut in pieces)
Romaine leaves
Paprika

Mash cheese with back of a spoon or fork until soft. Blend in sour cream until smooth. Stir in mayonnaise, salt, and cream. Makes about 1½ cups dressing.

Combine fruit with shrimp. Toss lightly. Arrange romaine leaves on each salad plate. Top with pineapple mixture. Spoon dressing over, and sprinkle with paprika. Makes 6 to 8 servings.

VEGETABLE
SALADS

A Vegetable Salad

is a year-round, all-occasion menu refresher. It brings crisp freshness to a winter meal, and delicious coolness to a summertime menu. It can perk up a family meal, and round out a barbecue or picnic menu. Some vegetable salads are hearty enough to be luncheon entrées; others are elegant enough to sparkle on a party buffet table.

A vegetable salad, of course, can be only as good as the vegetables that go into it. Select good quality fresh vegetables, and prepare them with care. Many vegetables—such as zucchini, cauliflower, broccoli, asparagus, mushrooms—which are usually cooked make delicious salad ingredients when served raw. Keep cooked vegetables on the tender-crisp side; never let them get soft and limp! Drain them immediately after cooking. Both raw and cooked vegetables should be chilled and crisp. If you want to use leftover buttered vegetables in a salad, dip them in hot water or hot meat stock to remove the butter (the stock will add flavor to your salad); then drain and chill them thoroughly.

Use imagination in combining salad vegetables. Many fresh and colorful combinations are possible—the only rule is to keep the ingredients harmonious in colors, textures, and flavors.

Mexican Salad Bowl

4 slices bread, cut in ½-inch cubes
1 tablespoon butter or margarine
1 clove garlic, minced or mashed
½ cup sliced celery
½ cup finely sliced onion, separated into rings
½ green pepper, sliced
½ cup shredded carrots
1 cup diced cooked potatoes
1 head of lettuce
⅓ cup salad oil or olive oil
¼ cup cider vinegar
1 teaspoon salt
Pepper to taste
2 teaspoons sugar
1 teaspoon chili powder
¼ teaspoon crumbled dried oregano
1 medium-sized avocado
Juice of 1 lime
½ cup stuffed green olives

Garlic croutons add crunchy bits of flavor to this mixed vegetable salad tossed with a chili-seasoned dressing.

Sauté bread cubes in butter with the garlic until bread is golden brown; drain on paper toweling. Mix together lightly the celery, onion, green pepper, carrots, potatoes, and the croutons; heap in a salad bowl lined with lettuce leaves. Blend together the salad oil, vinegar, salt, pepper, sugar, chili powder, and oregano. Pour over salad and toss lightly. Garnish the top with slices of avocado sprinkled with lime juice and with stuffed olives cut in half. Makes 8 servings.

Mixed Vegetable Salad

2 packages (10 oz. each) frozen mixed vegetables
Boiling salted water
2 tablespoons chopped parsley
2 green onions (including tops), chopped
¼ teaspoon seasoned salt
2 teaspoons vinegar
1 teaspoon dried dill seed
½ teaspoon sugar
½ cup mayonnaise
1 can (10½ oz.) asparagus tips, drained
Salad greens

Salads that wait are in demand for company as well as family meals. This one is actually improved by chilling awhile before serving time.

Cook the mixed vegetables in boiling salted water as directed on the package, except allow about 2 minutes less cooking time than is specified. Remove from heat, drain, and chill until about an hour before serving time. Blend in gently the parsley, green onions, seasoned salt, vinegar, dill seed, sugar, and mayonnaise. Let stand in the refrigerator for at least a half hour. Heap into a bowl lined with crisp greens. Arrange the asparagus tips on top as a garnish. Makes 6 to 8 servings.

Hearty Vegetable Salad

1 small cauliflower
Boiling salted water
¼ cup French dressing
2 cups shredded raw cabbage
1 package (10 oz.) frozen peas
or 1½ cups fresh peas, cooked
¼ pound fresh spinach, shredded
¼ cup finely minced onion
1 small carrot, grated
1 cup sliced celery
1 cup cooked frozen or fresh small
green lima beans
¼ teaspoon salt
Pepper to taste
½ cup each French dressing
and mayonnaise
Lettuce cups
Paprika

For eye appeal you vary the shape of the nine vegetables in this salad: some you cut in shreds or slices; others stay whole.

Cook cauliflower in boiling salted water until barely tender; drain and let cool. Separate into flowerets, and marinate in the ¼ cup French dressing, turning the cauliflowerets so they are well coated with dressing. Chill. Toss together lightly the cabbage, peas, spinach, onion, carrot, celery, lima beans, salt, and pepper to taste. Blend together the French dressing and mayonnaise and toss with the mixed vegetables, including the cauliflowerets. Pile into a lettuce-lined bowl and sprinkle with paprika. Makes 10 servings.

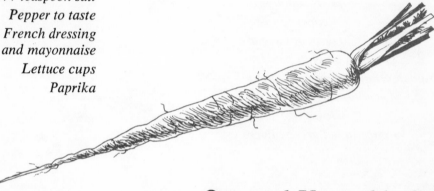

Oriental Vegetable Salad

¼ cup (4 tablespoons) salad
or olive oil
3 tablespoons tarragon vinegar
¼ cup (4 tablespoons) catsup
¼ cup (4 tablespoons) sugar
1 tablespoon lemon juice
½ teaspoon salt
¼ teaspon paprika
Pinch of garlic salt
½ pound fresh spinach
1 small can (6 oz.) bamboo shoots
1 small can (6 oz.) water chestnuts
1 medium-sized can (18 oz.)
bean sprouts
1 hard-cooked egg
2 tablespoons toasted sesame seeds
or crisp, crumbled bacon

Toasted sesame seeds, bamboo shoots, and water chestnuts give an Oriental air to this salad. The sharp dressing sets off the mild-flavored vegetables.

Gradually stir salad oil into vinegar; add the catsup, sugar, lemon juice, salt, paprika, and garlic salt, and stir thoroughly. Chill. Tear spinach into small pieces in salad bowl. Thinly slice bamboo shoots and water chestnuts, and place alternately with bean sprouts on bed of spinach. Stir dressing and pour over all. Sieve hard-cooked egg over salad and sprinkle with toasted sesame seeds. Makes 6 servings.

Tossed Vegetable Salad, Rancher's Style

½ head of lettuce
½ cucumber, peeled and thinly sliced
8 radishes, thinly sliced
1 tomato, cut in wedges
3 green onions and tops, sliced
1 cup (½ pint) commercial sour cream
½ cup small curd cottage cheese
¼ teaspoon salt
Pepper, garlic salt, and paprika

Although this salad starts out as a regular mixed vegetable salad, it ends up with a different flavor. Instead of tossing with a French dressing, you coat the greens with a cottage cheese and sour cream mixture.

Break the lettuce into small chunks and arrange in a salad bowl with the cucumber, radishes, tomato, and onions. Beat together lightly the sour cream, cottage cheese, and salt; add pepper, garlic salt, and paprika to taste. Pour dressing over lettuce mixture and toss. Makes 6 to 8 servings.

Mexican Fiesta Salad

1 head lettuce
1 large avocado
4 tomatoes, peeled and diced
1 green pepper, seeded and chopped
1 small onion, finely chopped
4 slices bacon
1½ teaspoons chili powder
½ teaspoon salt
⅓ cup cider vinegar

The name of this vegetable salad is suggested by its gay colors and the hot chili dressing.

Line a salad bowl with lettuce broken into small pieces. Cut avocado in half lengthwise, pit, peel, and slice; arrange slices petal-like around the edge of the salad bowl. Pile diced tomatoes in the center. Sprinkle with green pepper and onion. Fry bacon until crisp and crumble over all. Stir chili powder and salt into bacon drippings; stir in vinegar and pour hot over the salad. Serve immediately. Makes 6 to 8 servings.

Fruit-Vegetable Salad Plate

1 cup commercial sour cream
½ cup finely chopped chutney
2 tablespoons mayonnaise
¼ to ½ teaspoon Tabasco
Crisp lettuce leaves
1 pint (2 cups) cottage cheese
Few drops yellow food coloring (optional)
Choice of fruits and vegetables

A large and tantalizing salad plate for a buffet or a table centerpiece.

To make the dressing, combine sour cream with chutney, mayonnaise, and Tabasco to taste. Refrigerate until time to serve. Arrange lettuce leaves on a large salad plate or platter. Add a little yellow food coloring to the cottage cheese if you wish; mound in the center of salad plate.

Arrange fruits and vegetables around outside of the plate—pineapple slices, banana chunks, fresh or canned pear quarters, apple wedges, avocado slices, asparagus spears, tomato wedges, and cucumber slices. Pass the dressing separately. Makes 6 to 8 servings.

Italian Appetizer Salad

1 small head cauliflower
1 head each red lettuce, escarole,
and curly endive
1 can (1 lb.) each cut green beans,
red kidney beans, and garbanzos
2 or 3 green onions, chopped
6 hard-cooked eggs, sliced
1 cup olive oil
½ cup vinegar
1½ teaspoons salt
¼ teaspoon pepper
2 tomatoes, sliced
1 can (2¼ oz.) sliced ripe olives
1 or 2 cans (2 oz. each) anchovies
(rolled or fillets)

This salad, in a way, combines *antipasto* with greens. More than an "appetizer," it deserves an important place in the menu.

Break cauliflower into flowerets and parboil until just slightly tender; drain. Combine in large salad bowl the greens, three kinds of beans, green onions, and 4 of the eggs. Toss with dressing made with oil, vinegar, salt, and pepper. Garnish top with tomato slices, remaining egg slices, olives, and anchovies. Serve immediately. Makes 10 to 12 servings.

Asparagus Salad

2 pounds asparagus
½ cup soup stock or bouillon
½ teaspoon salt
2 or 3 onion slices
½ cup French dressing
1 small head lettuce
1 tablespoon chopped parsley
Fresh ground black pepper
Paprika

Snap the tough lower ends off asparagus; trim and wash. Bring the soup stock to a boil, add salt and onion slices. Cook the asparagus spears in the seasoned stock until just tender. Carefully remove asparagus from the cooking liquid and arrange in a shallow dish. Pour over it a well-seasoned French dressing. Turn occasionally while cooling. When well chilled, arrange the spears on shredded lettuce on individual salad plates. Sprinkle with freshly ground black pepper, paprika, and chopped parsley. If desired, arrange an anchovy strip or two over each portion of asparagus, and garnish each salad plate with tomato wedges and ripe or green olives. Makes 6 servings.

Bean Sprout and Water Chestnut Salad

Use fresh bean sprouts if you can find them—they are much crisper than the canned.

Clean sprouts well or drain the canned ones. To each 2 cups of sprouts, add ¼ cup sliced water chestnuts, ½ cup pineapple chunks, and ¼ cup slivered green pepper. For the dressing, combine 1 cup mayonnaise with 1 teaspoon *each* soy and curry powder. Mix the dressing through the salad. Arrange salad in lettuce-lined bowl. Sprinkle toasted almonds over the top. Makes 6 servings.

Marinated Artichokes

6 medium-sized artichokes
Boiling salted water
½ cup olive oil or salad oil
5 cloves garlic, minced or mashed
½ cup chopped fresh parsley
¼ cup lemon juice
½ teaspoon salt
Dash of pepper
Chicory or other salad greens

Wash artichokes thoroughly under running water. Cut off stems and remove coarse outer leaves. Also cut about 1 inch off the tops, cutting straight across with a sharp knife. Set in a large kettle with stem ends down. Cover with boiling water; cover pan and cook until tender, 30 minutes to 1 hour, depending on the size of the artichokes. Drain well and spread apart the leaves slightly. Combine the oil with garlic, parsley, lemon juice, salt, and pepper. Pour the oil mixture over the artichokes, and continue to pour through the artichokes until the leaves are well coated. Return artichokes to the pan and simmer them for 10 minutes in the oil mixture. Let stand at room temperature at least 1 hour before serving. Arrange on individual salad plates garnished with sprigs of chicory. Makes 6 servings.

Brussels Sprouts Salad

1½ pounds Brussels sprouts
Boiling salted water
1 cup mayonnaise
2 tablespoons chopped ripe olives
6 tablespoons chili sauce
1 tablespoon chopped onion
1 tablespoon vinegar
½ teaspoon minced parsley
Pinch of salt
1 hard-cooked egg, chopped
Romaine
1 tablespoon sliced pimiento

A Louis type of dressing—the type you serve over crab, shrimp, or lobster salad—suits a Brussels sprouts salad equally well.

Cook Brussels sprouts in a large amount of boiling salted water until tender. Drain and chill. For the dressing mix together the mayonnaise, chopped olives, chili sauce, onion, vinegar, parsley, salt, and chopped egg. Chill. Slice Brussels sprouts into ¼ to ½-inch thick slices. Pour over the dressing and mix lightly. Pile into a bowl lined with romaine and garnish with pimiento. Makes 6 servings.

Brussels Sprouts Slaw

2 pounds Brussels sprouts
2 eggs
½ cup commercial sour cream
2 tablespoons melted butter or margarine
3 tablespoons vinegar
1¼ teaspoons salt
Pepper

Wash and trim sprouts, removing the outside leaves. Place sprouts in ice water to crisp; drain thoroughly and cut crosswise in slices ⅛ inch thick; chill. Beat the eggs in a saucepan with sour cream and butter. Bring vinegar to a boil. Stirring, pour hot vinegar gradually into egg mixture; stirring, cook slowly until mixture is hot, but do not boil. Remove from heat, add salt and pepper to taste, then chill well.

When dressing is cold, pour over sliced sprouts and toss lightly. Chill until ready to serve. Makes 6 to 8 servings.

Celery Knob Salad Bowl

3 pounds (about 4 medium-sized)
celery roots
1 cup diced celery
½ cup chopped walnut meats
¼ cup seedless raisins
¼ cup minced chives
¼ cup finely chopped
green pepper
2 tablespoons stuffed green olives,
cut in halves
¾ cup mayonnaise
1 teaspoon salt
¼ teaspoon Tabasco
2 tablespoons tarragon vinegar
Dash freshly ground pepper
Escarole or chicory
1 cup (½ pint) commercial
sour cream
Paprika

This hearty salad looks like potato salad, but the white cubes are celery root; other ingredients include walnuts, raisins, and celery.

Scrub celery roots, cover with boiling water, cover the pan, and simmer about 25 or 30 minutes, until tender. Drain, cool, peel, and dice celery root. Combine with celery, nut meats, raisins, chives, green pepper, and olives. Dress with mayonnaise blended with salt, Tabasco, vinegar, and pepper; chill. Mound salad on crisp escarole or chicory in a salad bowl. Swirl sour cream on top and color with paprika. Makes 8 servings.

Celery Victor

2 small hearts of celery
1 medium-sized onion
2½ cups bouillon (10½ oz. can
diluted with 1 can water or 3 beef
bouillon cubes dissolved in 2½
cups hot water), or chicken stock
1 cup well-seasoned
French dressing
Water cress or shredded lettuce
Coarsely ground black pepper
Anchovy fillets and
pimiento strips
Tomatoes and ripe olives
(optional)

Chef Victor Hirtzler of the St. Francis Hotel in San Francisco first originated this now classic salad in the early 1900's.

Wash celery, trim the root end, and cut off all but the smallest leaves. Peel and slice onion. Put whole celery hearts and sliced onion in shallow pan; cover with bouillon. Cover and cook until tender, about 15 minutes. Let cool in stock. Remove hearts, cut in half lengthwise, and place in shallow dish. Pour over French dressing (a garlic-flavored French dressing made with wine vinegar is especially good), and chill several hours.

To serve, drain off most of dressing and place celery on water cress or shredded lettuce. Sprinkle with pepper and garnish with anchovy fillets and pimiento strips. Quartered tomatoes and ripe olives may be used for extra garnish. Makes 4 servings.

Raw Cauliflower Salad

1 small head cauliflower,
thinly sliced
3 unpeeled red apples, diced
1 cup sliced celery
3 small green onions, sliced
¾ cup chopped parsley, or 1 small
bunch water cress, chopped
1 clove garlic
½ teaspoon salt
¼ cup red wine vinegar
¼ cup salad or olive oil
Pepper to taste

Chill cauliflower, apples, celery, onions, and parsley or water cress thoroughly so they are very crisp. Rub salad bowl with cut clove of garlic and salt. Shake vinegar, oil, and pepper vigorously in a tightly covered jar. Pour over salad and toss lightly. Makes 6 servings.

Frosted Cauliflower Salad

1 head cauliflower
3 tablespoons wine vinegar
6 tablespoons olive oil
¼ teaspoon each salt and pepper
1 small clove garlic
2 avocados
2 ripe tomatoes
1 onion, finely chopped
Salt to taste

Mashed avocado, well seasoned, may be used to advantage to decorate a whole head of cauliflower which has been cooked just until tender and then chilled.

Cook whole head of cauliflower in salted water just until tender and no longer; chill. Shake together the vinegar, oil, salt and pepper; drop in garlic and let stand in dressing until just before using. Peel and mash avocados, peel and dice tomatoes, and combine with chopped onion. Add salt to taste and whip together until fluffy. Place chilled cauliflower on chop plate, garnish with crisp greens. Pour oil and vinegar dressing over cauliflower, then frost with avocado and tomato mixture. Makes 6 or more servings, depending on size of the cauliflower.

Tossed Cauliflower Salad

1 medium-sized head of cauliflower
½ cup French dressing
1 small avocado
½ cup sliced stuffed green olives
3 tomatoes, cut in eighths
½ cup Roquefort cheese, crumbled
Crisp greens

Separate cauliflower into flowerets; cover with ice water and chill 1 hour; drain. Chop cauliflower coarsely; pour over French dressing and let stand 2 hours. Just before serving, dice avocado and add to salad along with olives, tomatoes, and cheese. Toss lightly; serve on crisp greens. Makes 8 servings.

Tarragon Cucumbers

2 medium-sized cucumbers
1 teaspoon salt
⅓ cup fruit syrup from canned apricots
About ¼ cup tarragon vinegar
1 teaspoon sugar
½ teaspoon fresh tarragon or ¼ teaspoon dried tarragon
¼ teaspoon freshly ground black pepper
Salad greens
Sliced cucumbers for garnish

A touch of tarragon and sweetening makes this salad unusually refreshing. If you haven't syrup from canned apricots on hand, you can substitute peach or pear syrup.

Peel cucumbers. Slice very thinly into a bowl. (The slicing section of a grater is a good utensil.) Sprinkle salt over cucumbers. Place a weight on top of cucumbers. Allow to stand at room temperature for 6 to 8 hours. Occasionally drain off the juice that collects. Combine apricot syrup, vinegar, sugar, tarragon, and pepper. Taste and add a little more vinegar if dressing is too sweet. About 1 hour before serving, pour dressing over cucumbers; toss lightly. Place in refrigerator to chill thoroughly. At serving time, turn cucumbers into chilled shallow salad bowl lined with crisp greens. Garnish, if you wish, with a row of unpeeled sliced cucumbers. Makes about 4 servings.

Sliced Cucumber and Onion Salad

3 medium-sized cucumbers
2 tablespoons salt
1½ quarts ice water
1 sweet red onion
2 tablespoons salad oil or olive oil
2 tablespoons vinegar
Freshly ground pepper to taste

Cucumbers appear in a new guise here: they're sliced the long way with a vegetable peeler, so that each long paper-thin slice is rimmed with green peeling.

With a vegetable peeler, slice unpeeled cucumbers lengthwise into very thin slices. Soak in the salted ice water in the refrigerator for at least 1 hour. Then drain off all but 2 tablespoons of water. Peel onion, slice thinly, and separate into rings; toss with the cucumber slices. Sprinkle salad oil, vinegar, and pepper over all, and toss until vegetables are well coated with dressing. Serve immediately. Makes 6 to 8 servings.

Yogurt Cucumber Salad

2 medium-sized cucumbers
1 cup yogurt
4 teaspoons finely chopped fresh mint leaves or 1 teaspoon dry crushed mint leaves
Salt to taste

Mint, cucumber, and yogurt are united in this salad.

Peel cucumbers and slice very thinly. Blend yogurt with mint leaves and salt (add a touch of fresh garlic if desired). Toss cucumbers with yogurt dressing. Chill at least 1 hour before serving. Makes 4 or 5 servings.

Pea Salad

1½ cups cooked green peas
1 cup sliced celery
3 hard-cooked eggs,
coarsely chopped
½ cup mayonnaise
1 cup coarsely chopped
salted peanuts
3 tomatoes, sliced

Chopped salted peanuts top this colorful mixed vegetable salad.

Combine peas, celery, and chopped egg; chill. To serve, spoon pea mixture on 6 salad plates. Drop spoonfuls of mayonnaise over each salad, sprinkle with chopped peanuts, and garnish with tomato slices. Makes 6 servings.

Green and Gold Salad

3 cups cooked peas
½ cup diced Cheddar cheese
3 tablespoons minced onion
½ cup French dressing
1 tablespoon prepared mustard
Salad greens

To accompany this hearty luncheon salad, you might serve cold sliced meat or meat loaf, sliced tomatoes, deviled eggs, and corn bread sticks.

Toss together lightly the peas, cheese, and onion. Pour over the French dressing, mixed with the mustard, and toss lightly. Chill. Spoon into a salad bowl lined with greens. Makes 6 servings.

Near East Salad with Yogurt-Mint Dressing

1 cup each cooked green beans,
peas, and diced or sliced carrots
1 cup thinly sliced unpeeled
cucumbers
Crisp greens
Salt to taste
1 cup yogurt
⅓ cup light cream
1 tablespoon finely chopped
fresh mint leaves

Chill vegetables thoroughly. Arrange in separate stacks on 4 individual salad plates or in shallow bowls lined with crisp greens. Sprinkle lightly with salt. Blend yogurt with cream, and spoon on top of each salad. Sprinkle with the chopped fresh mint leaves. Makes 4 servings.

Dilled Green Pea Salad

2 packages (10 oz. each) frozen peas
3 tablespoons salad oil
1 to 2 tablespoons lemon juice
¾ teaspoon dill weed
¼ teaspoon basil
1 whole clove garlic
Salt and pepper to taste
1 cup thinly sliced celery
Lettuce
Hard-cooked egg slices

Cook peas as directed on package; drain, reserving ⅓ cup of the cooking water. Combine peas, the ⅓ cup cooking water, salad oil, lemon juice, dill weed, basil, garlic, salt and pepper. Chill. Discard garlic. Toss with celery. Serve from a lettuce-lined bowl; decorate with the hard-cooked egg slices. Makes 6 servings.

Hot Beans and Bacon

1 pound fresh green beans, cut up,
or 1 can (1 lb.) cut green beans,
drained
1 teaspoon salt
Dash pepper
⅓ cup salad oil
3 tablespoons catsup
2 tablespoons vinegar
½ cup halved radishes
2 slices crisp cooked bacon

Chilled fresh radishes add sharpness and color to this hot bean salad.

Cook fresh beans in boiling salted water until tender, about 15 minutes; drain. Mix together the 1 teaspoon salt, pepper, oil, catsup, and vinegar. Pour dressing over hot beans and radishes, and toss. Crumble bacon over top. Serve hot. Makes 4 servings.

Frosted Green Bean Salad

¾ cup salad or olive oil
6 tablespoons vinegar
Salt and pepper to taste
2 pounds cooked green beans,
split lengthwise
1 bunch green onions,
sliced ¼ inch thick
8 hard-cooked eggs
6 tablespoons mayonnaise
4 teaspoons vinegar
2 teaspoons prepared mustard
8 slices crisp cooked bacon
Salt to taste

This outstanding dish can double as salad and vegetable at a barbecue or buffet supper.

Shake together the oil, 6 tablespoons vinegar, and salt and pepper to taste; pour over the green beans and onions and let chill several hours. Just before serving, chop the hard-cooked eggs and mix with mayonnaise, vinegar, and mustard; crumble in the bacon and add salt to taste. Spoon egg topping over beans. Makes 8 servings.

Marinated Green Bean Salad

2 cans (1 lb. each)
red kidney beans
2 cans (about 1 lb. each)
whole green beans
2 cans (about 1 lb. each)
yellow wax beans
2 cans (about 1 lb. each) garbanzos
2 large green peppers, cut into
thin rings
1 large fresh red pepper, cut
into thin rings
5 medium-sized sweet salad onions,
cut into thin rings
1 cup sliced pimiento-stuffed olives
1 can (4 oz.) pimientos, diced
¾ cup each salad oil, white vinegar,
and sugar
Crisp romaine leaves

Our taste testers judged this bean salad highly flavorsome, crisp and light. For quickest preparation, use high quality canned green and wax beans; but for best flavor, use fresh beans if they're in season.

Turn thoroughly drained kidney beans, green beans, wax beans, and garbanzos into a large container for marinating. Add green and red peppers and onions; sprinkle with olive slices and pimiento bits, reserving a few for garnish; mix all lightly. Shake together in a covered jar the salad oil, vinegar, and sugar. Pour over bean mixture. Cover and marinate in refrigerator at least 6 hours before serving. At serving time, line a large wooden salad bowl with romaine leaves. Turn in bean mixture. Garnish with reserved sliced olives and pimiento. Makes 20 servings.

Kidney Bean Salad

2 cans (1 lb. each) red kidney
beans, drained
1 cup sliced celery
1 green pepper, chopped
1 dill pickle, diced
½ cup olive oil
½ cup red wine vinegar
¼ cup (4 tablespoons each)
chopped parsley and green onions
½ clove garlic, mashed or minced
1 tablespoon capers
1 teaspoon each minced fresh basil
and tarragon
½ teaspoon chili powder
1 teaspoon sugar
Few drops Tabasco
½ teaspoon salt
Salad greens, sliced radishes,
tomato wedges
Freshly ground pepper

Tender and mild kidney beans, in combination with crisp vegetables and a sharp dressing, make a hearty salad.

Mix together kidney beans, celery, green pepper, and dill pickle; chill. Just before serving, combine olive oil, wine vinegar, parsley, green onions, garlic, capers, basil, tarragon, chili powder, sugar, Tabasco, and salt; pour over salad mixture, then toss together gently. Arrange mixture on greens and garnish with sliced radishes and tomato wedges. Grind black pepper over salad before serving. Makes 8 servings.

Salami and Bean Salad

1 clove garlic (optional)
2 sprigs parsley, minced
½ small onion, chopped fine
1 small head lettuce, torn in bits
1 tomato, cut in small pieces
¼ cup canned red kidney beans
Salt and pepper
4 thin slices salami
French dressing

Whether or not you rub your salad bowl with garlic depends on the strength of the salami you are using in this salad. Use wine vinegar in your French dressing to add extra zip.

Rub salad bowl with cut clove of garlic, if desired. Combine parsley, onion, lettuce, tomato, and kidney beans in salad bowl and sprinkle with salt and pepper. Cut salami in long thin strips and toss into salad. Pour French dressing over and toss thoroughly. Makes 4 servings.

Cranberry Bean Salad

2 cups dried cranberry beans
6 cups water
2 teaspoons salt
½ cup red wine vinegar
1 cup sliced celery
½ cup chopped green onions and tops
½ cup chopped green pepper
Lettuce cups

Cooked cranberry beans are chilled for this mixed vegetable salad. Vinegar blends with the sauce for a slightly tart dressing.

Wash the beans, then place in a large kettle with the water; cover, bring to a boil, and cook 2 minutes. Remove from heat and let soak 1 hour before cooking again. Add the salt, bring to a boil, and cook 2 hours, or until tender. Drain the beans and stir in the vinegar; chill. To serve, add the celery, green onions and tops, and green pepper; mix lightly. Serve in lettuce cups. Makes 6 to 8 servings.

Tossed Lima Bean Salad

1½ packages (10 oz. each) frozen baby lima beans
1 cup sliced celery
1 dill pickle, diced
4 green onions and tops, chopped
¾ pound bologna, cut in strips 1 inch long and ¼ inch thick
½ cup commercial sour cream
4 tablespoons (¼ cup) mayonnaise
2 tablespoons lemon juice
2 teaspoons horse-radish mustard
Crisp greens for garnish

Cook beans in boiling salted water 16 to 18 minutes, or until tender; drain and chill. Combine the chilled limas, celery, dill pickle, onions, and bologna. Blend together until smooth the sour cream, mayonnaise, lemon juice, and horse-radish mustard. Pour dressing over lima bean mixture, toss, and chill. When ready to serve, line a large chop plate or 8 individual plates with crisp greens. Spoon salad on greens. Makes 8 servings.

Full Meal Salad

1 package (10 oz.) frozen
lima beans, cooked

1 clove garlic, minced or mashed

½ cup tart French dressing

1 teaspoon dry mustard

¼ teaspoon paprika

½ teaspoon Italian
mixed dried herbs

Salt

3 green onions and tops, sliced

4 radishes, sliced

1 to 1½ cups ham strips

½ cup slivered Cheddar cheese

Lettuce cups

Mayonnaise

Lima beans, marinated in well-seasoned French dressing, make a flavorful salad base for ham and cheese strips.

Mix limas with garlic, French dressing, mustard, paprika, herbs, and salt to taste. Chill. Toss lima beans with the green onions, radishes, and ham and cheese strips. Spoon into a bowl lined with lettuce, and garnish with mayonnaise. Makes 4 servings.

Mushroom and Lima Bean Salad

1 package (10 oz.) frozen
lima beans

8 sliced fresh mushrooms or 1 can
(4 oz.) sliced mushrooms, drained

1 large onion, chopped

1 tablespoon chopped fresh parsley
or 1 teaspoon dry parsley flakes

½ teaspoon oregano

⅓ cup wine vinegar

3 tablespoons olive oil

1 clove garlic, minced or mashed

½ teaspoon salt

¼ teaspoon celery salt

¼ teaspoon pepper

Onion rings

Here lima beans benefit from a chilling in a spicy French dressing marinade.

Cook lima beans according to package directions until tender. Drain, rinse under cold running water, and drain thoroughly again. Toss together with mushrooms, onion, parsley, and oregano.

In a covered jar or container, shake together vinegar, olive oil, garlic, salt, celery salt, and pepper. Pour over bean mixture and toss thoroughly. Chill in refrigerator 1 to 2 hours. To serve, heap into casserole lined with crisp salad greens. Garnish with thinly sliced onion rings. Makes 4 servings.

Sweet-Sour Kidney Bean Cabbage Slaw

1 can (1 lb.) red kidney beans
3 cups shredded cabbage
¼ cup chopped sweet pickles
¼ cup sliced green onions
½ cup golden raisins
½ teaspoon celery seed
⅓ cup chili sauce
½ cup mayonnaise
Salt to taste

This is a tasty, one-dish substitute for a crisp cabbage cole slaw and a baked bean casserole. Try it served with hot dogs or ham slices grilled over the open coals.

Drain and chill kidney beans. Toss together with cabbage, sweet pickles, green onions, raisins, celery seed, and a dressing made by combining the chili sauce and mayonnaise. Salt to taste. Makes 6 servings.

Slaw à l'Anchois

4 tablespoons olive oil
1 can (2 oz.) anchovy fillets in olive oil
4 tablespoons vinegar
1 clove garlic, thinly sliced
1 medium-sized head cabbage
4 strips bacon, cooked until very crisp

Heat olive oil over medium heat. Add can of anchovies, including oil in which they are packed. Add vinegar and stir with fork until anchovies break apart. Add thinly sliced garlic and let simmer over low heat for 5 minutes.
  Shred cabbage into long, thin shreds. Pour hot dressing over. Mix and divide into individual servings. Crumble bacon over each serving. Makes 4 to 6 servings.

Walnut Cabbage Salad

1 small head cabbage
1 avocado, cubed
1 carrot, grated
1 cup chopped walnuts
4 green onions, sliced
Garlic salt to taste
½ cup mayonnaise
2 tablespoons prepared mustard
Juice of 1 lemon

This is a colorful cabbage salad with the yellow-green of avocado, the orange of carrots, the bright green of crisp onions, plus the additional crispness of walnut pieces.

Finely shred cabbage and mix with avocado, carrot, walnuts, green onions, and garlic salt. Blend mayonnaise, mustard, and lemon juice, then add to vegetables and toss. Makes 6 servings.

Lemon Slaw

6 cups finely shredded
white cabbage
2 unpeeled red apples, diced
½ cup each chopped green pepper
and green onions
1 teaspoon sugar
⅓ cup dry white table wine

This mixture of cabbage, red apple, green pepper, and onion is very colorful, crisp, and piquant.

Toss cabbage, apples, green pepper, and green onions with sugar; add wine; toss, and chill. Combine with this dressing: Mix together 3 hard-cooked egg yolks, 1 teaspoon dry mustard, 1 tablespoon sugar, 2 tablespoons salad oil, 1 teaspoon salt, pepper to taste, 1 teaspoon grated lemon peel, ½ cup lemon juice; fold in ½ cup whipping cream, beaten stiff. Makes 8 to 10 servings.

California Slaw

1 small head cabbage
2 tart apples, chopped
1 medium-sized onion, minced
2 pimientos, minced
3 hard-cooked eggs
¼ teaspoon salt
1 tablespoon sugar
1 teaspoon dry mustard
1 tablespoon butter, melted
⅓ cup vinegar
½ cup cream, whipped

A good choice for a quiet family dinner, this slaw would be equally at home at a party buffet. The dressing is based on hard-cooked egg yolks, beaten smooth and folded into whipped cream.

Shred cabbage and combine with apples, onion, and pimientos. Rub yolks of eggs to a paste and add salt, sugar, mustard, and butter. Mix well. Slowly add vinegar, beating thoroughly. Fold in cream. Combine with cabbage mixture and garnish with sliced egg whites and parsley. Makes 6 servings.

Grape Cole Slaw

1 medium head cabbage,
finely shredded
1 carrot, shredded
1 cup green grapes, seeded
½ cup light raisins, plumped
in orange juice
Salt
2 tablespoons sugar
¼ cup mayonnaise
2 tablespoons tarragon vinegar
¼ teaspoon curry powder

In five minutes you can assemble this fruity slaw. Grapes and white raisins, plus a dash of curry, make it a children's favorite. For extra eye appeal, serve it on a bed of crinkly dark green Savoy cabbage.

Combine the finely shredded cabbage with shredded carrots, grapes, and the raisins plumped in orange juice. Sprinkle with salt to taste, and sugar. For the dressing, blend the mayonnaise with the tarragon vinegar and curry powder. Add dressing to cabbage mixture and toss lightly. Garnish the bowl with lettuce leaves, if you wish. Makes 8 servings.

Tropical Cabbage Salad

1 medium-sized head cabbage
1 cup flaked coconut
¾ cup commercial sour cream
2½ tablespoons vinegar
¾ teaspoon salt
¼ teaspoon pepper
1 tablespoon sugar
Toasted coconut
Paprika

Finely shred cabbage. Add flaked coconut. Blend together sour cream, vinegar, salt, pepper, and sugar. Toss lightly with cabbage and coconut. Sprinkle with toasted coconut and paprika. (To toast coconut, spread a thin layer on a baking sheet and toast in a 350° oven for 3 or 4 minutes, watching carefully and stirring when necessary.) Makes 6 to 8 servings.

Beet and Curry Salad

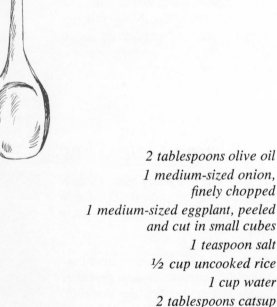

½ cup vinegar
¼ cup salad oil
1 teaspoon sugar
Salt, pepper, and curry powder
to taste
1 can (1 lb.) diced beets, drained
½ cup chopped onion
Lettuce cups

The strength of the curry powder you use determines the amount (about ½ teaspoon, or stronger to taste).

In a jar with a cover, mix vinegar, salad oil, and sugar; add salt, pepper, and curry powder. Shake well. Combine beets, onion, and dressing. Mix well, and let chill several hours. Spoon into lettuce cups. Makes 4 servings.

Mediterranean Salad

This stuffed pepper salad combines some unusual flavors. You might serve it with cold ham slices.

2 tablespoons olive oil
1 medium-sized onion,
finely chopped
1 medium-sized eggplant, peeled
and cut in small cubes
1 teaspoon salt
½ cup uncooked rice
1 cup water
2 tablespoons catsup
2 green peppers

Heat the oil in a medium-sized saucepan. Add the onion and eggplant cubes; cook for about 5 minutes, or until soft. Add the salt, rice, and water. Cover and cook over low heat until the rice is tender. Stir in the catsup. Cut the peppers in halves, remove the seeds and veins, and fill with the rice mixture. Place in a baking dish, and pour about ¼ cup water in the bottom of the pan. Bake in a moderate oven (350°) for 30 to 40 minutes, or until the peppers are tender, but still firm. Chill. Serve cold topped with mayonnaise sauce. Makes 2 to 4 servings.

MAYONNAISE SAUCE:
Combine ½ cup mayonnaise with 2 tablespoons sweet pickle relish and 3 tablespoons lemon juice.

Green Pepper Ring Salad

Endive and shredded lettuce
2 green peppers, cut in thin rings
2 medium-sized onions, thinly sliced
½ cup tart French dressing

You have to enjoy the crispness and sharpness of green pepper and onion rings to appreciate this combination.

Line 6 salad plates with endive and shredded lettuce; arrange alternate rings of green pepper and onion on greens. Before serving, pour a little tart French dressing over each salad. Makes 6 servings.

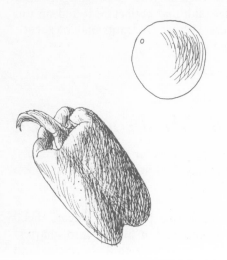

Orange and Green Pepper Salad

Cut the peel from 6 oranges, so that all white is removed, and cut in slices ⅓ inch thick. Arrange in overlapping rows on a platter, surround with lettuce leaves, and top with 1 sweet onion and 1 green pepper, sliced so thin they are transparent. (You'll need a sharp knife for this. Or, if you'd rather, just chop the onion and pepper very fine.) Arrange on top of the oranges, pour on a cup of French dressing, and chill thoroughly before serving. Makes 12 servings.

Eggplant Salad

1 medium-sized eggplant
2 green onions, chopped
3 medium-sized fresh tomatoes,
cut in cubes
¼ cup cider vinegar
3 tablespoons salad oil
1½ teaspoons salt
Freshly ground pepper to taste
½ teaspoon sugar

Here is an interesting new way to enjoy eggplant. Combined with bright red tomatoes, it makes a colorful and unusual salad. As an extra advantage, it's a salad that you can make ahead of time, then leave to marinate in the refrigerator for several hours.

Wash the eggplant and set it on a baking sheet without peeling it. Bake in a moderately hot oven (375°) for about 45 minutes, or until tender when pierced with a fork. Peel when it is cool enough to handle; chill in your refrigerator. Cut the eggplant into cubes. Mix it with onion, tomatoes, vinegar, salad oil, salt, pepper, and sugar. Chill for several hours to marinate the vegetables. Serve on lettuce. Makes 4 to 6 servings.

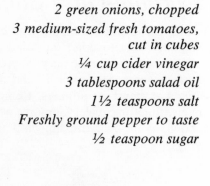

Hearts of Palm

Cut canned palm pieces in half lengthwise. Pour over them wine vinegar or red table wine and olive oil. Sprinkle with plenty of freshly ground pepper and garnish with pimiento slivers. Chill for a few hours before serving.

Brazilian Heart of Palm Salad

Arrange sliced lettuce on individual plates; sprinkle with salt, pepper, a little lemon juice, and minced chives. Top each with half a peeled ripe tomato. Chop water cress, allowing ¼ cup (packed) for each serving, and mix with 2 tablespoons chopped heart of palm and just enough French dressing to hold together (use 3 parts light salad oil to 1 part lemon juice, salt and pepper). Mound on top of each tomato and serve. (Water chestnuts may be substituted for the heart of palm.)

Fresh Mushroom Salad

½ pint (1 cup) commercial
sour cream
1 tablespoon lemon juice
1 teaspoon each salt and sugar
1 small carton (¼ lb.) mushrooms,
thinly sliced
2 green onions, sliced
1 head iceberg lettuce
2 hard-cooked eggs, grated

Raw fresh mushrooms, sliced wafer-thin, add their distinctive flavor to this creamy, tart dressing that you spoon over wedges of head lettuce.

Mix together sour cream, lemon juice, salt, sugar, sliced mushrooms, and green onions. Cut lettuce into quarters and arrange on 4 plates. Spoon over chilled dressing and sprinkle with grated egg. Makes 4 servings.

Mushroom-Olive Salad

1 teaspoon salt
1 tablespoon water
1 clove garlic, minced
⅔ cup salad oil
¼ cup vinegar
2 teaspoons lemon juice
1 teaspoon sugar
½ teaspoon each dry mustard,
rosemary, and Worcestershire
1 can (4 oz.) button mushrooms,
drained
1 medium-sized head lettuce,
torn in shreds
½ cup sliced celery
3 green onions and tops, chopped
1 tablespoon minced parsley
¼ cup stuffed green olives, sliced

Dissolve salt in water; add garlic and let stand for at least 30 minutes; stir occasionally. Mix together the salad oil, vinegar, lemon juice, sugar, mustard, rosemary, Worcestershire, and drained mushrooms. Strain garlic and add garlic water to dressing. Let stand 20 minutes. Remove mushrooms and arrange with lettuce, celery, onions, parsley, and olives in a bowl; pour over dressing and toss lightly. Makes 6 servings.

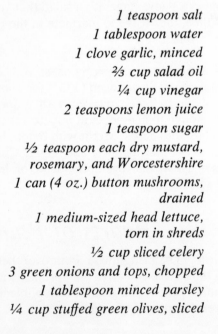

Kohlrabi Salad Niçoise

2 cups peeled, coarsely
shredded kohlrabi
¼ cup sliced radishes
3 tablespoons mayonnaise
1 teaspoon sugar
2 tablespoons each vinegar
and salad oil
½ teaspoon dry mustard
Salt and pepper to taste
Lettuce cups
Paprika

Toss kohlrabi and radishes with a mixture of the mayonnaise, sugar, vinegar, salad oil, mustard, salt, and pepper. Chill for several hours. Serve in crisp lettuce cups, sprinkled with a little paprika. Makes 3 or 4 servings.

Potato Salad with Sour Cream

2 pounds new potatoes
1 teaspoon sugar
1 teaspoon salt
½ teaspoon dry mustard
Freshly ground pepper
¼ cup vinegar
2 teaspoons caraway or dill
seed (optional)
1 cucumber, sliced
2 cups (1 pint) commercial
sour cream
Lettuce
Paprika or finely minced, sweet
red pepper

A well-chilled, robust potato salad is always a favorite. Here is an especially good version.

Boil potatoes; peel and slice thin. Mix together sugar, salt, mustard, pepper, vinegar, caraway or dill seed, cucumber, and sour cream. Combine with potatoes; chill. Put in a lettuce-lined bowl, and sprinkle with paprika or red pepper. Makes about 6 servings.

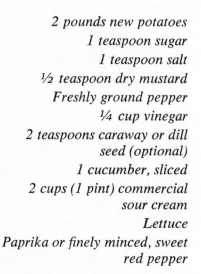

French Potato Salad

The tart, peppery seasoning in this salad distinguishes it from the standard potato salads. Try this with steak in place of the traditional French fries.

Cook 8 small, round red potatoes in their skins until tender. Without peeling, slice potatoes thinly. Peel and slice very thinly one Bermuda onion; separate into rings. In shallow dish place alternate layers of the sliced potatoes and onion rings; salt and pepper each layer and sprinkle chopped parsley bits over it. Make French dressing with 2 tablespoons white wine vinegar and 3 tablespoons salad oil. Pour dressing over layers of potato and onion and refrigerate salad overnight. Turn mixture at least once to make sure salad is well coated with the marinade. Makes about 5 servings.

Curried Potato Salad

6 large potatoes
½ cup tart French dressing
4 hard-cooked eggs, chopped
1 cup sweet Bermuda onion, chopped
1 cup celery, chopped
1 small green pepper, finely chopped
2 cups mayonnaise
2 tablespoons curry powder
½ to ¾ teaspoon salt
Romaine leaves

The day before, bake potatoes in a very hot oven (450°) about 1 hour or until tender. Remove skins when they are cool enough to handle. Cover and allow to cool completely. Slice potatoes into a large bowl; sprinkle thoroughly with the French dressing. Cover and store in the refrigerator. Chop eggs, onion, celery, and green pepper; store in separate containers in refrigerator. Blend ¼ cup of the mayonnaise with the curry powder and salt; then stir in remaining mayonnaise. Several hours before serving combine potatoes, eggs, onion, and celery. Fold mayonnaise into potato mixture and arrange in a bowl lined with romaine leaves. Garnish with the chopped green pepper. Makes 16 servings.

Hot Potato and Bacon Salad

4 cups cooked potatoes (4 medium-sized potatoes), cut in ½-inch cubes
16 slices bacon, cooked and crumbled
1 cup chopped green onions and tops
½ teaspoon salt
Dash of pepper
1½ cups mayonnaise
¼ cup (4 tablespoons) prepared mustard
¼ cup (4 tablespoons) prepared horse-radish
1 cup sliced celery
¼ cup finely chopped carrots
Paprika

Mix together lightly the cubed potatoes, crumbled bacon, green onions, salt, and pepper. Combine the mayonnaise, mustard, and horse-radish in a saucepan; heat, stirring constantly, until sauce bubbles; stir in the celery and carrots. Pour the hot sauce over potato mixture and toss lightly. Sprinkle paprika over top and serve immediately. Makes 8 generous servings.

Hot Cheese-Potato Salad

4 cups peeled and cubed
cooked potatoes
2 hard-cooked eggs, chopped
½ cup sliced celery
⅓ cup minced onion
2 tablespoons minced green pepper
⅓ cup cider vinegar
1½ teaspoons salt
1 teaspoon dry mustard
¼ teaspoon pepper
2 slices bacon, diced
2 cups (½ lb.) shredded sharp
Cheddar cheese

This interesting winter version of potato salad has a broiled Cheddar cheese topping. For a flavor variation, add 1 small can sliced ripe olives.

In a large bowl, mix together the potatoes, eggs, celery, onion, and green pepper. Sprinkle with vinegar, salt, mustard, and pepper. Sauté bacon until crisp; pour hot drippings and crisp bacon over potato mixture and toss lightly. Turn into a shallow baking pan and sprinkle with cheese. Place under the broiler until the cheese is bubbly. Makes 8 servings.

Cottage Cheese-Potato Salad

1 cup (½ pint) creamed
cottage cheese
½ cup mayonnaise
1 tablespoon lemon juice
1 teaspoon dry mustard
1½ teaspoons salt
⅛ teaspoon pepper
3 cups cooked, diced potatoes
½ cup thinly sliced celery
2 tablespoons onions, finely chopped
1 tablespoon each chopped green
pepper and chopped pimiento
Crisp greens

Potato salad has a different texture when bound together with a mayonnaise-cottage cheese mixture. Bits of green pepper and pimiento brighten its appearance.

Mix together cottage cheese, mayonnaise, lemon juice, mustard, salt, and pepper. Lightly toss with potatoes, celery, onions, green pepper, and pimiento. Chill thoroughly. Serve in individual lettuce cups or in a salad bowl lined with greens. Makes 6 servings.

Tomatoes in Sweet-Sour Dressing

4 to 5 large, firm, ripe tomatoes
½ cup red or white wine vinegar
¼ cup water
1½ tablespoons sugar
2 tablespoons finely chopped
green onions and tops
Freshly ground pepper

Here, the tang of wine vinegar contrasts with the sweetness of tomatoes.

Peel tomatoes and cut crosswise in thick slices; arrange on a serving platter. Mix together the vinegar, water, sugar, and chopped onions; pour over tomatoes. Grind pepper to taste over all. Chill at least 1 hour. Makes 6 servings.

East Indian Salad

12 tomatoes, peeled
2 cups mayonnaise
2 tablespoons curry powder
2 teaspoons lemon juice
12 minced anchovies
1 cup cleaned, cooked shrimp,
cut in pieces
1 cup ripe olives, pitted
1 envelope (1 tablespoon)
unflavored gelatin
¼ cup cold water
Parsley

These piquant stuffed tomatoes add an interesting touch to a holiday buffet.

Scoop out centers from tomatoes, and turn upside down to drain. Combine mayonnaise, curry powder, lemon juice, anchovies, shrimp, and olives. Soften gelatin in the cold water and melt over hot water. Add gelatin to shrimp mixture. Spoon into tomatoes and chill thoroughly; garnish tops with parsley. Makes 12 servings.

Garlic Tomatoes

Chilled, garlic-seasoned, sliced tomatoes are an especially good accompaniment for barbecued shortribs, steaks, or hamburgers. Scald and peel 5 large tomatoes; cut in ⅓-inch-thick slices. Place a single layer of the sliced tomatoes on a chop plate.

To 1½ cups French dressing, add 1 or 2 cloves of garlic, mashed or minced. Pour some of the dressing mixture over tomatoes; sprinkle with crumbled dried oregano, salt, and pepper. Add another layer of tomato slices, and repeat dressing, oregano, salt, and pepper. Continue until all tomato slices are used. Cover chop plate with foil and chill for at least 3 hours. Makes 8 servings.

Stuffed Tomato Casserole Salad

2 cups diced cooked potatoes
1 cup small Swiss cheese cubes
⅔ cup diced bologna
1 small onion, finely chopped
Salt and pepper to taste
½ cup sharp French dressing
6 large tomatoes
Mayonnaise
Paprika
Lettuce

This is not the usual stuffed tomato salad. Cubes of Swiss cheese, bologna, and potato blend with the zippy onion seasoning.

In a large bowl, combine potatoes, Swiss cheese cubes, bologna, onion, salt, and pepper. Mix lightly with French dressing. Remove stem ends from tomatoes. With a sharp knife, slash from top halfway down each tomato, in about 6 places. Spread tomato open. Fill with potato mixture. Top with a spoonful of mayonnaise, and a dusting of paprika if desired. Serve in lettuce-lined individual casseroles. Makes 6 servings.

Bean Sprout-Stuffed Tomatoes

6 medium-sized, firm, ripe
tomatoes
1 medium-sized can (1 lb. 4 oz.)
bean sprouts, drained and chopped
1 small green pepper, finely chopped
1 sprig parsley, finely chopped
2 stalks celery, sliced
½ teaspoon salt
¼ teaspoon pepper
¼ teaspoon celery salt
¾ cup mayonnaise
Paprika
Salad greens

Crisp celery and rather bland bean sprouts combine well with tomato to make a colorful salad.

Cut out stem end of tomatoes and scoop out the pulp, leaving firm shells; chill. Drain off excess juice from pulp and combine with bean sprouts, green pepper, parsley, celery, salt, pepper, celery salt, and mayonnaise. Stuff tomato shells with salad mixture and shake paprika over top. Arrange on crisp greens. Makes 6 servings.

Tomato, Orange, and Anchovy Salad

4 tomatoes
4 oranges
Lettuce
2 cans (2 oz. each) anchovy fillets
½ cup sliced stuffed olives
⅓ cup olive oil
¼ cup wine vinegar
½ teaspoon salt
Freshly ground pepper

Peel and thinly slice tomatoes and oranges (choose ones of equal size). Arrange slices alternately on a tray of lettuce or on individual salad plates. Decorate with anchovy fillets and olives. Sprinkle with dressing made by shaking together oil, vinegar, salt, and pepper. Makes 8 servings.

Sliced Tomatoes with Mustard Dressing

1 cup cider vinegar
3 eggs
⅔ cup sugar
2 tablespoons flour
1 teaspoon dry mustard
½ teaspoon salt
¼ teaspoon pepper
¼ cup whipping cream
8 medium-sized, firm, ripe tomatoes
Shredded lettuce
1 tablespoon mustard seeds

Mustard—in powdered form in the dressing and as seeds on top—spices this tomato salad.

Heat vinegar to scalding. Beat eggs until blended; mix together sugar, flour, and mustard and beat into the eggs. Stir in salt and pepper. Gradually add the hot vinegar to the egg mixture and beat until blended. Cook over low heat, stirring for 2 minutes. Cool. When ready to serve, whip cream and fold in. Peel and slice tomatoes; arrange them on shredded lettuce on a large chop plate. Spoon dresssing over the tomatoes and sprinkle mustard seeds over all. Makes 10 generous servings.

Sauerkraut-Stuffed Tomatoes

12 medium-sized, firm, ripe tomatoes
Salt and pepper to taste
6 tablespoons salad oil
¼ cup (4 tablespoons) lemon juice
2 tablespoons sugar
¼ teaspoon paprika
⅛ teaspoon salt
1 large can (1 lb. 13 oz.)
sauerkraut (3½ cups)
Romaine or other crisp salad greens

The sharp acidity of sauerkraut makes an interesting flavor contrast to sun-sweet tomatoes in this salad.

Peel tomatoes, cut off stem end, and scoop out most of pulp, leaving a thick shell; turn upside down to drain. Sprinkle the tomato cavities with salt and pepper to taste. Mix together the oil, lemon juice, sugar, paprika, and the ⅛ teaspoon salt. Pour dressing over sauerkraut and toss lightly. Spoon sauerkraut mixture into tomato cavities; chill tomatoes for about 1 hour. Arrange stuffed tomatoes on salad greens. Makes 12 servings.

Vegetable Salad with Zucchini

½ head lettuce
1½ cup thinly sliced raw zucchini
½ cup sliced celery
1 cup thinly sliced raw carrots
2 green onions and tops, chopped
5 radishes, sliced
1 tablespoon chopped parsley
¼ teaspoon salt
½ cup mayonnaise
⅓ cup tarragon or wine vinegar

Crisp wheels of raw zucchini are tossed with other vegetables in this combination salad. If you wish, embellish the basic salad dressing with salad herbs.

Shred lettuce and toss with the zucchini, celery, carrots, green onions and tops, radishes, and parsley. Sprinkle with salt. Mix together mayonnaise and vinegar and toss thoroughly until vegetables are coated with dressing. Makes 6 servings.

MEAT, POULTRY & SEAFOOD SALADS

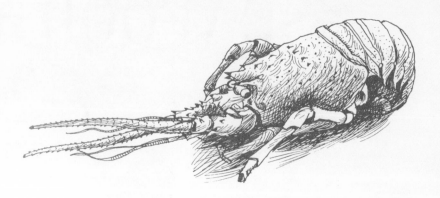

Meat, Fish and Poultry

salads are the hearty members of the salad family. They are usually served as full-meal salads, the mainstay of a luncheon or supper—but in small servings, many of them are excellent appetizer salads.

You will find some famous salads in this group. The Crab Louis on page 84 has become a classic salad that is served in many restaurants, and the Louis dressing now appears on other seafood salads as well. The Cobb Salad on page 82 is another old favorite; and on page 89, prawns are dressed with a version of the famous Green Goddess Salad Dressing (see page 20).

Salads in this chapter make wonderful use of leftovers. Chunky bits of leftover chicken, for example, become impressive enough for a party luncheon when they are combined with orange-colored apricot slices, bits of green onion, and crisp water chestnuts. Creamy cottage cheese and crunchy celery stretch leftover ham into a main dish salad with delightful texture contrasts.

Most of the salads that follow here have one thing in common: they make use of crisp, crunchy ingredients—green pepper, cucumber, pickle, nut meats, celery, water chestnuts—to offset the smoother, heavier textures of meat, fish, and poultry.

Beef or Veal Salad

2 tablespoons tomato paste
½ teaspoon prepared horse-radish
3 tablespoons vinegar
2 tablespoons meat broth or fat-free meat juices
2 cups thinly sliced lean beef or veal (from roast or broiled steak cooked rare)
Salt and pepper
Salad greens (part water cress, if desired)
Radishes

Here's a hearty meat salad enriched by an almost-no-calorie dressing.

Blend together tomato paste, horse-radish, vinegar, and meat stock. Toss with meat. Season to taste with salt and pepper. Let chill at least 1 hour. Serve on a bed of mixed salad greens and garnish with decoratively cut radishes. Makes 4 to 6 servings.

Veal and Bacon Salad

6 medium-sized tomatoes
1 teaspoon salt
Lettuce cups
3 cups diced, cooked veal
½ cup sliced celery
½ cup crumbled, crisp bacon
¼ cup sliced radishes
¾ cup mayonnaise

Cold leftover veal can be used in this hearty salad. The cubed meat, crisp vegetables, and bacon are spooned into sectioned tomato cups.

Peel tomatoes and cut in 6 sections—but not all the way through—so they will open like a flower; sprinkle with salt. Arrange in lettuce cups; chill. Toss together the veal, celery, bacon, and radishes; mix in the mayonnaise. Spoon salad into tomato shells. Makes 6 servings.

Ham Slaw

½ cup commercial sour cream
2 tablespoons mayonnaise
2 to 4 tablespoons crumbled blue cheese
2 tablespoons finely chopped green pepper or green onion
⅛ teaspoon salt
1 tablespoon wine vinegar
4 cups finely shredded cabbage
1 thinly sliced large apple
1 to 2 cups ham, cut in cubes or thin strips

Blue cheese flavors this hearty cabbage and ham salad, a good choice for a luncheon.

Blend sour cream, mayonnaise, cheese, green pepper or green onion, salt, and vinegar. Chill several hours. In a large salad bowl, put cabbage, apple, and ham. Pour dressing over salad and toss gently. Makes 6 to 8 servings.

Ham-Vegetable-Cottage Cheese Salad

½ cup diced or slivered cooked ham
½ cup sliced celery
¾ cup cooked peas
¾ cup pitted ripe olives, sliced
1 cup cottage cheese
2 tablespoons mayonnaise
½ teaspoon salt
Salad greens
Paprika

In this main dish salad, you get a wide range of colors as well as flavors. The creamy cottage cheese provides a smooth background for the crunch of celery.

Mix together the ham, celery, peas, and sliced olives. Combine the cottage cheese, mayonnaise, and salt, and toss together with the ham and vegetable salad mixture. Heap in a salad bowl lined with greens or spoon into lettuce cups for individual salads. Sprinkle the top with paprika. Makes 4 generous servings.

Ham and Sausage Salad Bowl

1 can (2¼ oz.) deviled ham
1 can (4 oz.) Vienna sausages
1 small head lettuce
1 bunch water cress
1 small bunch radishes
1 cucumber
4 green onions
½ cup French dressing
(not too salty)

Deviled ham and Vienna sausages are spicy accents in this salad that is almost a meal in itself.

Chill ham and sausages well; cut ham in small cubes, and slice sausages in ½-inch lengths. Break the lettuce and water cress into small pieces and place in a salad bowl. Slice radishes, cucumber, and green onions; arrange on top of lettuce, along with deviled ham and sliced sausages. Pour over French dressing and toss. Makes 6 servings.

Supper Salad

1½ cups diced cooked ham, pork, veal, or turkey
½ cup diced cooked potatoes
½ cup sliced cooked carrots
½ cup each cooked peas and green lima beans
½ cup cooked green beans, cut in 1-inch lengths
1 cup French dressing
½ cup chopped sweet pickle
2 hard-cooked eggs, chopped
¾ cup mayonnaise
Salt, pepper, and paprika
Crisp salad greens

Here's the "build-up" technique—meat, eggs, potatoes, and colorful cooked vegetables.

Place the ham, potatoes, carrots, peas, lima beans, and green beans in a bowl; pour over French dressing, toss lightly, and chill for at least 1 hour. When you are ready to serve, add the pickle, eggs, and mayonnaise; mix lightly. Season to taste with salt, pepper, and paprika. Serve on crisp greens. Makes 6 servings.

Buffet Salad Bowl

1 head lettuce
2 large tomatoes, quartered
2 hard-cooked eggs, halved
1 cup cubed luncheon meat
½ cup American cheese,
cut in strips
6 green onions, chopped
Burgundy Dressing (see below)

Shred lettuce coarsely. Arrange in salad bowl with tomatoes, eggs, meat, and cheese on top. Sprinkle with the chopped onion. Before serving, toss all ingredients together with Burgundy Dressing. Makes 4 or 5 servings.

BURGUNDY DRESSING:
1 teaspoon salt
1 teaspoon sugar
¼ teaspoon dry mustard
Dash pepper
2 tablespoons grated onion
½ cup Burgundy
¼ cup cider vinegar
¼ cup salad oil

Measure ingredients in the order given into a jar and shake until well blended. Makes 1 cup dressing.

Frankfurter Club Salad

6 regular-size frankfurters
2 tomatoes
2 cups cooked lima beans
1 cup Swiss, jack, or Cheddar
cheese cubes
Club Salad Dressing (see below)
6 strips crisp cooked bacon
2 to 3 cups torn crisp lettuce

Cut frankfurters in ½-inch diagonal slices. Cut tomatoes into eighths. Arrange frankfurters, tomatoes, limas, and cheese in separate piles in a large salad bowl. Pour over half the Club Salad Dressing. Marinate in refrigerator several hours. When ready to serve, coarsely crumble bacon into bowl, add lettuce, and toss with additional dressing until ingredients are well coated. Makes 6 to 8 servings.

CLUB SALAD DRESSING:
½ cup salad oil
⅓ cup wine vinegar
3 green onions, chopped
1 small clove garlic,
minced or mashed
¼ teaspoon paprika
½ teaspoon dry mustard
¾ teaspoon salt
¼ teaspoon dill seed

Shake all ingredients together in a covered jar until blended. Makes 1 cup.

Skillet Frankfurter Salad

5 or 6 hot cooked potatoes
2 stalks celery
5 radishes
6 slices crisp cooked bacon
1 small head lettuce
1 cup cooked peas
Hot Skillet Dressing (see below)
3 hard-cooked eggs, sliced
Crisp lettuce leaves

Reminiscent of German hot potato salad, this full-meal salad has a delicious sweet-sour dressing.

Peel and cube potatoes. Slice celery and radishes, and break bacon into large pieces. Tear lettuce into bite-sized pieces. Toss all together gently with peas and Hot Skillet Dressing. Heap back into the warm skillet. Garnish top with hard-cooked eggs and around edge with lettuce leaves. Makes 6 to 8 servings.

HOT SKILLET DRESSING:
Boiling water
6 regular-size frankfurters
1 small onion, finely chopped
¼ cup bacon drippings
2 tablespoons flour
1 cup chicken broth
⅓ cup vinegar
1½ teaspoons salt
Few grains pepper
1 teaspoon celery seed
1 tablespoon sugar

Pour boiling water over frankfurters and let stand 5 minutes. Sauté onion in bacon drippings until soft but not browned. Blend in flour. Add broth slowly; cook and stir until smooth and thickened. Stir in vinegar, salt, pepper, celery seed, and sugar. Cook 5 minutes more. Drain the frankfurters, slice, and add to dressing.

Corned Beef-Potato Salad

1½ cups diced cooked potatoes
½ cup finely sliced celery and leaves
¼ cup chopped sweet pickle
1 teaspoon grated onion
1 cup cubed corned beef (half of a 12-oz. can)
½ cup mayonnaise or salad dressing
1 teaspoon prepared mustard
3 tablespoons chili sauce
¼ teaspoon salt
Dash of pepper

In this hearty salad, a well-seasoned, spicy dressing binds cubed corned beef and potatoes together.

Combine potatoes, celery, pickle, onion, and corned beef. Blend mayonnaise, mustard, chili sauce, salt, and pepper; pour over potato mixture and toss lightly. Chill thoroughly. Garnish, if desired, with crisp lettuce leaves, tomato wedges, and carrot curls. Makes 4 servings.

Sweetbread Salad with Grapes

Wash 3 pounds of sweetbreads and cook in acidulated water (add juice of ½ lemon and 1 teaspoon salt to each quart) for 20 minutes. Drain and plunge them into cold water; when cold remove membrane and dark spots, and cut in pieces the size of grapes. Cover with ½ cup French dressing and chill. When ready to serve, combine with 3 cups seedless (or halved and seeded) grapes, 2 cups minced celery, and 1½ cups mayonnaise. Mix gently, add salt and more mayonnaise if necessary, chill, and serve from a large bowl. Makes about 12 servings.

Hearty Chef's Salad

½ cup French dressing
1 cup French style green
beans, cooked
1 cup 2-inch carrot sticks, cooked
1 cup 2-inch raw celery sticks
1 medium-sized head of lettuce
1 cup cooked ham slivers,
cut ¼ inch thick
½ cup Swiss cheese strips,
cut ¼ inch thick
2 hard-cooked eggs, sliced
¾ cup mayonnaise
¼ cup (4 tablespoons) chili sauce
2 tablespoons horse-radish

Pour French dressing over green beans, carrot sticks, and celery sticks; toss lightly and chill for 2 hours; drain. Break lettuce into eight pieces and arrange around the edge of a large salad bowl. Pile drained vegetables, ham slivers, and cheese strips in the center of the bowl; arrange egg slices around the vegetable mixture. Beat together until smooth the mayonnaise, chili sauce, and horse-radish; spoon over salad and serve immediately. Makes 8 servings.

Salade de Maison

3 tomatoes
1 whole cooked chicken breast
3 anchovy fillets
2 hard-cooked eggs
1 bunch water cress
1 head iceberg lettuce
French dressing
Curry powder

Peel tomatoes, discard juice and seeds, and chop the pulp. Remove skin from chicken and cut the meat in small cubes. Chop the anchovy fillets, hard-cooked eggs, and water cress. Cut the lettuce in small chunks. Combine the tomatoes, chicken, anchovy fillets, hard-cooked eggs, water cress, and lettuce in a large bowl. Pour over enough French dressing—seasoned with curry powder to taste—to moisten salad, and toss. Makes 6 servings.

Chicken Salad Piquant

2 large whole chicken
breasts (about 1 lb.)
1 cup water
1 teaspoon salt
2 tablespoons white wine vinegar
1 teaspoon grated orange peel
2 green onions, thinly sliced
(including part of the tops)
2 large oranges, peeled and
thinly sliced
Salt and pepper
Salad greens

The dressing for this flavorful chicken and orange salad has only about 2 calories per tablespoon.

In a small saucepan, combine chicken, water, and salt. Bring to a boil; cover and simmer slowly 15 to 20 minutes, or until chicken is tender. Let cool in stock. Strain and save stock. Discard skin and bones and cut meat in thin strips or thin slices. Mix together ½ cup chicken stock, vinegar, orange peel, and green onions. Pour this dressing over chicken. Add oranges. Chill 1 hour. Season with salt and pepper; serve on salad greens. Makes 4 to 6 servings.

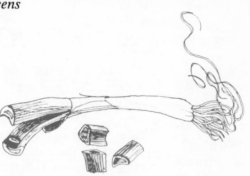

Chicken Breast Salad

6 whole, boned chicken breasts
1 small package (3 oz.)
cream cheese
¼ cup mayonnaise
2 teaspoons lemon juice
¼ teaspoon grated lemon peel
Dash of salt
1 finely chopped green
onion and top
Crisp lettuce
2 or 3 large tomatoes,
peeled and chilled
Salt and pepper
2 large avocados
½ cup toasted slivered almonds
(optional)
Pitted ripe olives

Cook chicken breasts until tender (you can either pan-fry them in butter, covered to keep them moist, or simmer them in broth). Chill breasts. Remove skin and pat dry. Mix together thoroughly the cream cheese, mayonnaise, lemon juice, lemon peel, salt, and onion.

Coat rounded side of each piece of chicken completely with cheese dressing. Arrange crisp lettuce on 6 dinner-sized plates. Cut tomatoes into 6 thick slices and place on lettuce. Sprinkle with salt and pepper. Arrange a coated chicken breast on each tomato slice. Halve and peel avocados, and cut each half into 3 slices; place 2 avocado slices on each plate. Sprinkle chicken with toasted almonds and garnish with ripe olives. Makes 6 servings.

Apricot Chicken Salad

1½ cups diced cooked chicken
1½ cups sliced fresh apricots
1 cup thinly sliced
water chestnuts or celery
1 tablespoon finely chopped
green onion
¼ cup commercial sour cream
¼ cup mayonnaise
1½ tablespoons lemon juice
Salt to taste
Crisp lettuce

Bits of green onion and orange apricot slices among chunks of chicken make this salad pretty enough for a special luncheon. For a different way to serve it, you might heap the salad on a bed of crisp chow mein noodles rather than into lettuce cups.

Toss together lightly the chicken, apricots, water chestnuts, green onion, sour cream, mayonnaise, lemon juice, and salt. Serve in crisp lettuce cups. Makes 4 to 5 servings.

Chicken-Curry Salad

4 to 5 cups cooked chicken or
turkey, in large chunks
2 teaspoons grated onion
1 cup celery, cut in diagonal slices
1 cup finely chopped green pepper
¼ cup light cream
⅔ cup mayonnaise or salad dressing
1 teaspoon salt
⅛ teaspoon pepper
1 teaspoon curry powder
2 tablespoons vinegar
Salad greens

To heighten the delicate curry flavor, let this blend for several hours in the refrigerator.

Combine the chicken with onion, celery, and pepper. For the dressing, mix cream with mayonnaise, salt, pepper, curry, and vinegar. Add dressing to the chicken and toss lightly. Refrigerate until time to serve. Arrange the salad in a serving bowl or on individual plates; surround with crisp salad greens. Makes 6 to 8 servings.

Chilean Corn and Chicken Salad

2 ears of cooked corn
1 cup diced cooked chicken
1½ cups chopped peeled tomatoes
1 green pepper, seeded and
chopped
1 cup mayonnaise
½ teaspoon chili powder
Salt and pepper
Red lettuce, romaine, and stuffed
green olives for garnish

Cooked corn is good in salads. Run the knife close to the cob so you don't split the corn kernels.

With a sharp knife, cut the cooked corn kernels from the cob. Mix together the corn, chicken, tomatoes, green pepper, mayonnaise, and chili powder. Season with salt and pepper to taste; chill. To serve, arrange on a chop plate or individual salad plates lined with red lettuce and romaine; spoon corn mixture in the center; garnish with olives. Makes 4 to 6 servings.

Chicken and Avocado Tostado de Luxe

4 corn tortillas
Fat for frying
1 can (15 oz.) chili with beans
6 cups shredded lettuce
1 can (7 oz.) green chili sauce,
chilled
1 cup shredded Parmesan cheese
12 thin slices cooked chicken
2 avocados, peeled and sliced
Tomato wedges, radishes, olives,
green onions to garnish

This is similar to a basic tostado, but the chicken and avocado are added embellishments. You can garnish this tostado also with other fresh raw vegetables of your choice or with pickles or canned peppers.

In hot deep fat or shallow fat, fry tortillas (one at a time) until very crisp. Center on serving plates. Heat chili; spoon on top of crisp tortillas. Toss shredded lettuce with about half of the green chili sauce; pile in a stack over hot chili and in a bed around tortillas. Sprinkle 2 tablespoons of the cheese over each serving. Arrange chicken and avocado slices on top of the lettuce stacks; spoon remaining chili sauce over chicken and avocado. Sprinkle with the remaining cheese. Garnish with tomato wedges, radishes, olives, and green onions. Makes 4 tostados.

Crunchy Chicken Salad

1 cup mayonnaise
1½ teaspoons prepared mustard
About 2 tablespoons sweet
pickle juice
Salt and freshly ground black
pepper to taste
6 cups cooked chicken cut in chunks
4 cups sliced celery (including
a few tender leaves)
¼ cup chopped green pepper
¼ cup grated mild onion
1 large cucumber, diced
8 sweet pickles, diced
Coarsely shredded lettuce
Large, pitted ripe olives
2 large firm tomatoes, sliced
4 hard-cooked eggs, sliced
Paprika

This chicken salad is full of crunchy celery, cucumbers, and pickles, as well as big chunks of chicken; it's as hearty as it is crisp and refreshing.

Mix mayonnaise and mustard; add enough pickle juice to thin to a desired consistency. Add salt and pepper. Pour dressing over chicken, celery, green pepper, onion, cucumber, and pickles in a large mixing bowl. Toss lightly.

At serving time, turn salad into a large salad bowl lined with shredded lettuce. Garnish with olives, tomato slices, and egg slices. Sprinkle the egg slices with paprika. Makes 12 servings.

Cauliflower Chicken Salad

1 cup chopped cooked chicken
1 small head (3 cups finely chopped) raw cauliflower
¼ cup sliced pimiento-stuffed green olives
¼ cup finely chopped parsley
¼ cup chili sauce
2 tablespoons mayonnaise
1 tablespoon vinegar
2 teaspoons olive oil
1 teaspoon salt
½ teaspoon pepper

Fresh crisp cauliflower serves as a base for this colorful chicken salad. Serve individually in lettuce cups with a garnish of mayonnaise and a dash of paprika.

Combine chicken, cauliflower, olives, and parsley in large bowl. Mix thoroughly. Blend together chili sauce, mayonnaise, vinegar, olive oil, salt, and pepper; stir into salad; and toss thoroughly. Chill. Makes 6 to 8 servings.

Chicken Salad on Roquefort Romaine

4 whole, cooked chicken breasts
1 cup sliced celery
2 tablespoons finely sliced green onions
1 tablespoon each mustard and lemon juice
½ teaspoon salt
Freshly ground pepper to taste
Dash of cayenne
Roquefort dressing
4 slices bacon
4 cups broken romaine leaves
Lemon wedges, sliced stuffed olives, and parsley sprigs for garnish

Cut chicken from bone, then cut into good-sized chunks. Toss with celery, green onions, mustard, lemon juice, salt, pepper, cayenne, and enough Roquefort dressing to moisten (about ½ cup). Chill thoroughly. Cook bacon until very crisp; drain, crumble, and set aside. Toss broken romaine leaves with Roquefort dressing to coat. Arrange romaine leaves in bottom of 4 chilled salad bowls. Top each with a mound of chicken salad. Sprinkle with bacon crumbles. Garnish with lemon wedges, sliced stuffed olives, and parsley sprigs. Makes 4 servings.

Turkey Salad in Pineapple Shells

6 cups cubed cooked turkey
3 cups coarsely chopped walnut meats
2 cups sliced celery
1 teaspoon salt
3½ cups mayonnaise
1 large pineapple

A scooped-out pineapple shell makes a festive bowl for this turkey-nut salad.

Mix together the turkey, nut meats, celery, salt, and mayonnaise. Cut the pineapple in half lengthwise and cut out the meat. (To keep the salad cold on the table, freeze the shells before filling with the salad.) Fill the pineapple half shells with turkey salad and arrange on a large chop plate. Garnish with a few pieces of the fresh pineapple. Makes 12 servings.

Condiment Chicken Salad with Avocado and Greens

1½ cups mayonnaise
1 cup raisins
1 cup salted peanuts
1 cup mango chutney, cut into slivers
1 cup flaked coconut
2 pounds cooked chicken meat,
    diced coarsely
2 cups diagonally sliced
    ripe bananas
Salt and pepper to taste
Salad greens
Additional sliced bananas
Avocado slices
Lemon juice

This unusual chicken salad is so delicious you'll probably want to serve it on special occasions, perhaps as the entrée for a buffet salad luncheon. It's rich with chicken meat and curry condiments. To plump the raisins, let them stand in white wine a few hours before making the salad. Drain thoroughly.

Mix together the mayonnaise, raisins, peanuts, chutney, and coconut. Toss with chicken meat. Gently combine with sliced bananas. Season with salt and pepper. Mound into large lettuce bowl or on a platter lined with shredded lettuce and lettuce leaves. Garnish with slices of avocado and banana, which you have dipped into lemon juice. Makes 12 servings.

Cobb Salad

1 large head lettuce
1 bunch water cress
3 hard-cooked eggs
12 slices crisp cooked bacon,
    crumbled (1 cup)
⅓ cup crumbled Roquefort
    or blue cheese
4 medium-sized tomatoes, peeled
2 medium-sized avocados
2 boned cooked chicken breasts
1 tablespoon chopped chives
Butter lettuce
French dressing

This interesting salad was created quite by accident over 30 years ago by Robert H. Cobb, then owner of the Little Hat Derby, forerunner of the Brown Derby restaurants in the Los Angeles area.

Using the large blade of a food chopper or a French knife or cutting tool, coarsely chop the lettuce, water cress leaves (omit stems), hard-cooked eggs, bacon, cheese, tomatoes, avocados, chicken, and chives. Line plates with butter lettuce and pile salad on the plates, peaking it up. Garnish with olives, radishes, and avocado slices, if desired. Pass the dressing. Makes 4 servings.

Nun's Salad

Here is a good way to use up bits of cold turkey. Combine 3 cups cold boiled rice with enough mustard-flavored French dressing to moisten well, then gently fold in 1 cup (or more) of cold turkey cut in julienne pieces. Heap in a lettuce-lined bowl and sprinkle the top with a small can of minced ripe olives. Makes 4 to 6 servings.

Exotic Luncheon Salad

2 quarts coarsely cut cooked turkey

1 large can (20 oz.) water chestnuts

2 pounds seedless grapes

2 cups sliced celery

2 to 3 cups toasted slivered almonds

3 cups mayonnaise

1 tablespoon curry powder

2 tablespoons soy

Boston or bibb lettuce

1 large can (20 oz.) litchi nuts or
1 large can (1 lb. 13 oz.)
pineapple chunks

This salad is elegance itself. Chunks of pineapple can be used in place of the litchi nuts.

Use turkey breast meat. You will need 2½ to 3 pounds. Coarsely cut the turkey meat from bone into bite-size pieces.

Slice or dice the water chestnuts, and mix them with the turkey meat. Wash the grapes, pick them from their stems, and add, along with the celery and 1½ to 2 cups of the toasted almonds. Mix the mayonnaise with the curry powder and soy. (You may like a couple of tablespoons of lemon juice with it, too.) Combine with the turkey mixture, chill for serveral hours, then spoon into nests of Boston or bibb lettuce. Sprinkle with the remaining toasted almonds and garnish with the litchi nuts or pineapple chunks arranged on top of each serving. This recipe makes 12 generous servings. It can be easily multiplied to serve a larger group.

Fruited Turkey Salad

6 or 8 large slices cooked turkey

1½ cups cubed cooked turkey

1 cup chopped apple or celery

½ cup seeded grapes or canned
seedless grapes, drained

½ cup pineapple chunks,
fresh or frozen

¼ cup pomegranate seeds

¼ cup commercial sour cream

¼ cup mayonnaise

1 tablespoon lemon juice

½ teaspoon grated lemon peel

1 teaspoon grated onion

½ teaspoon salt

Few grains cayenne pepper

This salad is a mixture of fresh fruit and turkey, served in individual cornucopias formed with turkey slices—or with ham slices, if you prefer.

To make the cornucopias, roll the turkey slices into cone shapes; fasten the narrow end with a cocktail pick. For the filling toss together cubed turkey, apple (or celery), grapes, pineapple, and pomegranate seeds. Blend remaining ingredients; add to fruit mixture. Toss lightly. Makes enough filling for 6 to 8 cornucopias. Garnish salad platter with water cress or shredded lettuce.

Abalone Salad

1 can (5¼ oz.) cubed abalone
1 cup thinly sliced celery
¼ cup chopped green onions,
including some of the tops
6 radishes, thinly sliced crosswise
½ cup diced green pepper
¼ cup chopped pimiento
7 or 8 green olives, chopped
Mayonnaise (about ½ cup)
6 lettuce cups
Hard-cooked eggs

This salad contains chunks of richly flavored canned abalone, tossed with a combination of red and green vegetables, and mounded in crisp lettuce cups. It would make an unusual first course for a company meal.

Toss together abalone cubes, celery, green onion, radishes, green pepper, pimiento, and green olives with mayonnaise to moisten. Arrange lettuce cups on a chop plate, or individual serving dishes, and fill with abalone salad. Garnish with hard-cooked egg slices. Makes 6 servings.

Crab Louis

1 cup mayonnaise
¼ cup whipping cream
¼ cup chili sauce
¼ cup chopped green pepper
¼ cup chopped green onion
Salt to taste
Lemon juice to taste
2 heads iceberg lettuce
2 large Dungeness crabs, cracked
and shelled, or 1½ to 2 pounds
crab meat
4 large tomatoes
4 hard-cooked eggs

Which Louis originated this hearty, full-meal salad, we do not know, but Solari's Grill in San Francisco was among the first restaurants to serve it, around 1911. Now it is a favorite in many restaurants. The Louis dressing is good on shrimp, too.

Mix together the mayonnaise, whipping cream, chili sauce, green pepper, and green onion. Season with salt and lemon juice to taste. Arrange outer leaves of lettuce on 4 large plates; shred the heart of the lettuce and arrange a bed of shredded lettuce in the center of the leaves. Place the body meat of the crabs on the shredded lettuce. Cut tomatoes and eggs in sixths and arrange symmetrically around the crab. Pour over the Louis dressing, and garnish with crab legs. Makes 4 servings.

Crab and Artichoke Salad with Sour Cream Dressing

Place a thick wedge of crisp head lettuce on each of 8 individual salad plates. Blend together 1 cup commercial sour cream, 2 tablespoons minced chives, and the juice of 1 lemon. Cut in small pieces 1 jar (about 6 oz.) marinated artichoke hearts; add to sour cream mixture with oil marinade. Season to taste with salt. Spoon an equal amount on each serving of lettuce. Garnish each with 1 or 2 crab legs (or instead, blend 1 cup flaked crab meat with dressing). Makes 8 servings.

Coconut Crab Salad

1 medium-sized grapefruit
1 medium-sized avocado
4 cooked artichoke hearts
½ head iceberg lettuce, shredded
½ cup flaked coconut
1 pound (2 cups) crab meat
½ cup mayonnaise
2 tablespoons dry white table wine
3 tablespoons lemon juice
½ teaspoon salt
Pepper to taste
Lettuce

Peel grapefruit and lift segments out of membrane into salad bowl (reserve a few for garnish). Peel avocado, and slice (set aside a few slices and sprinkle with lemon juice). Add to bowl. Slice 2 artichoke hearts into bowl (save 2 for garnish). Add shredded lettuce, coconut, and crab meat. Mix together dressing of mayonnaise, wine, lemon juice, salt, and pepper. Pour about half over ingredients in salad bowl. Toss lightly. Heap salad into 6 lettuce-lined bowls; garnish with remaining grapefruit sections, avocado slices, and artichoke slices. Pass remaining salad dressing. Makes 6 servings.

Pineapple with Crab Salad

Cut the fruit from 1 pineapple into 6 slices; cut out the cores. On each of 6 salad plates, arrange crisp water cress or small tender spinach leaves. Set a pineapple slice on each. Then arrange 4 or 5 crab legs on each slice of pineapple (you'll need ¾ to 1 pound fresh, frozen, or canned crab). Serve with the following dressing. Makes 6 servings.

ROSY LIME DRESSING:
Combine ½ cup catsup with ¼ cup fresh lime juice (or you may prefer lemon juice); blend until smooth.

Oyster Salad

1 cup tarragon vinegar
3 cups water
1 teaspoon salt
1 teaspoon tarragon
2 pints oysters
1 cup mayonnaise
1 teaspoon lemon juice
1 tablespoon anchovy paste
1 teaspoon grated onion
Salt and white pepper to taste
1 large bunch celery
Anchovy fillets and stuffed green olives

If you serve generous portions of this salad, it makes an ideal main dish for a luncheon. Or serve it to accompany baked ham or tongue, perhaps at a guest buffet.

Combine tarragon vinegar with water, salt, and tarragon. Bring to a boil. Add oysters and cook for about 2 minutes, or just until the oysters plump and begin to curl on the edges. Drain oysters and chill thoroughly. Mix mayonnaise with lemon juice, anchovy paste, and onion. To serve, mix half of mayonnaise mixture with the oysters; season with salt and pepper. Slice celery very fine and make a bed of it on a platter or individual plates. Mound oysters on top, top with remaining mayonnaise mixture, and garnish with anchovy fillets and olives. Makes 4 main dish servings or about 8 smaller servings.

Oyster and Tomato Salad

½ cup water
1 tablespoon vinegar
½ teaspoon salt
Freshly ground pepper
1 pint (2 cups) medium-sized oysters
6 thick tomato slices
Lettuce
1 cup mayonnaise
2 teaspoons anchovy paste
1 teaspoon lemon juice

Heat to boiling the water, vinegar, salt, and a dash of freshly ground pepper. Add oysters; poach gently for about 3 minutes. Chill, and drain. For each serving, place a slice of tomato on lettuce, top with oysters. Serve with anchovy mayonnaise made by blending the mayonnaise, anchovy paste, and lemon juice. Makes 6 servings.

Sardine Salad

1 can (4½ oz.) sardines
1 hard-cooked egg
¼ cup finely chopped green onions,
    tops and all
½ cup finely sliced celery
1 cup chilled cooked peas
Mayonnaise
Lettuce
Paprika, sliced stuffed olives,
    lemon wedges

The onions and celery in this hearty salad mellow the decisive flavor of the sardines and add desirable crispness. Chives may be substituted for the green onions.

Chop sardines and hard-cooked egg together. Stir in green onions, celery, and peas. Mix with enough mayonnaise to hold together. Chill. Serve in mounds on lettuce. Sprinkle with paprika. Garnish with stuffed olives and serve with lemon wedges and mayonnaise. Makes 4 to 6 servings.

Sardine Vegetable Salad

1 cup diced cooked potatoes
1 cup diced cooked beets
2 cans (3 or 4 oz. each) sardines,
    drained
1 small onion, finely chopped
½ cup mayonnaise
Lettuce cups
Parsley and lemon wedges

The sardines break into bite-size pieces when you toss them with diced potatoes and beets in this full-bodied salad.

Toss together the potatoes, beets, sardines, and onions with the mayonnaise. Arrange in crisp lettuce cups. Garnish with parsley and lemon wedges. Makes 5 servings.

Crunchy Salmon Salad

½ cup salad dressing or mayonnaise
¼ teaspoon salt
⅛ teaspoon pepper
2 tablespoons lemon juice
1 tablespoon grated onion
½ cup light cream
1 can (1 lb.) salmon, drained and flaked
¼ cup diced sweet pickles
½ cup sliced celery
2 cups crushed potato chips
Lettuce cups

To insure that this salad will deserve its name, do not add the potato chips until a minute or two before serving; they rapidly soak up the moisture in the dressing.

Blend together salad dressing, salt, pepper, lemon juice, and grated onion. Stir in cream. Fold in drained salmon, pickles, and celery. Chill thoroughly. Just before serving, mix in potato chips. Shape into mounds on lettuce cups. Serve at once. Makes 4 to 6 servings.

Scallop Salad

1 pound scallops
1 quart (4 cups) water
1 tablespoon lemon juice
1 teaspoon salt
¾ cup mayonnaise
1 cup sliced celery
2 tablespoons chopped dill pickle
¼ teaspoon paprika
Lettuce
Hard-cooked egg quarters and tomato wedges for garnish

Try to assemble this salad ahead of time so the flavors will have a chance to blend.

Simmer scallops in water seasoned with the lemon juice and the 1 teaspoon salt for 8 to 10 minutes, or until tender; drain and chill. When cold, cut scallops into bite-size pieces. Combine with mayonnaise, celery, pickle, and paprika. Toss, taste, and add additional salt if desired. To serve, spoon onto 6 plates lined with lettuce, and garnish with egg quarters and tomato wedges. Makes 6 servings.

Shrimp and Bean Sprout Salad

1 pound fresh bean sprouts
2 green onions (including tops), minced
1 cup cut-up cooked shrimp or crab meat
1 cup yogurt
1 teaspoon curry powder
Pressed garlic
1 or 2 tablespoons lemon juice
2 tablespoons soy
Sugar, if desired

In the Orient, preparation of bean sprouts always includes removing the hair-like root. If you're short of time, however, this is not really necessary.

Prepare bean sprouts by pinching off and discarding the hair-like root. Combine with green onions and shrimp. Toss with yogurt mixed with curry, a little garlic, lemon juice, soy, and sugar to taste. Makes 4 or 6 servings.

Shrimp and Rice Salad

¼ cup uncooked white rice or
¾ cup cooked rice
1 cup cleaned, cooked shrimp
¾ teaspoon salt
¾ cup chopped raw cauliflower
1 tablespoon chopped stuffed
green olives
¼ cup slivered green pepper
¼ cup lemon juice
2 tablespoons French dressing
⅓ cup mayonnaise
1 tablespoon chopped onion
Pepper to taste
Lettuce cups

Shrimp, rice, and green pepper are a favorite trio in hot dishes. Here they are chilled together in a salad, and their textures and flavors are equally pleasing.

Cook rice according to any preferred method until tender; cool. Toss together lightly the cooked rice, shrimp, salt, cauliflower, stuffed green olives, and green pepper. Blend together thoroughly the lemon juice, French dressing, mayonnaise, onion, and pepper to taste. Pour dressing over salad and toss. Spoon into lettuce cups. Makes 4 servings.

Curried Shrimp

Shuck, clean, and cook shrimp in court bouillon; combine with dressing (1 cup mayonnaise, ½ cup chili sauce, 1 tablespoon curry powder, 1 to 2 tablespoons lemon juice). Serve on endive, chicory, or romaine, and sprinkle with chopped salted almonds.

Shrimp-Stuffed Artichokes

8 large artichokes
Boiling salted water
Tart French dressng
⅓ cup mayonnaise
1 tablespoon lemon juice
1½ cups cooked, cleaned shrimp
⅓ cup pitted ripe olives, sliced
1½ cups diced celery
Salt
Pepper
Paprika

Overflowing the centers of these artichokes is a colorful shrimp salad. If you like artichokes chilled, these should suit your fancy.

Wash artichokes; cut off tips and stem ends, and pull off tough outer leaves. In a covered saucepan, steam artichokes in 2 inches of boiling salted water for 35 to 45 minutes, or until tender. Drain; turn artichokes upside down to cool. Gently spread the outer leaves to form a cup, and using a teaspoon, scoop out the choke. Cover each artichoke with French dressing, and chill.

When ready to serve, combine mayonnaise and lemon juice, and toss lightly with shrimp, olives, and celery. Heap into drained artichoke cups, and sprinkle with salt, pepper, and paprika. Serve chilled. Makes 8 servings.

Shrimp Vegetable Salad

1 clove garlic
4 tablespoons (¼ cup) butter
4 slices day-old bread
1 package (10 oz.) frozen peas
cooked and chilled
1 cup cleaned, cooked small shrimp
4 tablespoons (¼ cup) mayonnaise
1 tablespoon light cream
1 tablespoon lemon juice
2 whole green onions, finely sliced
2 pinches sweet basil
Salt
Shredded lettuce

The most interesting part of this recipe is the unusual texture contrast of compact shrimp, tender peas, and crunchy garlic croutons.

Rub a bowl well with a cut clove of garlic. Then mash or mince remaining garlic and mix with melted butter in a small frying pan. Remove bread crusts and cut bread in small ½-inch cubes. Brown cubes in the garlic butter over a low heat, tossing until light brown and all the butter has been absorbed; cool. Combine peas, shrimp, mayonnaise, cream, lemon juice, onions and tops, and sweet basil. Salt to taste. Stir in garlic croutons just before serving. Serve on shredded lettuce. Makes 4 servings.

Prawn Salad with Green Goddess Dressing

2 pounds uncooked prawns or
large shrimp
1 quart celery pieces
Green Goddess Dressing
Parsley

The night before, shell and devein prawns. Put prawns in a large saucepan, cover with water and bring to a boil. Remove immediately from heat. Allow to cool for 15 minutes. Rinse in cold water and cut each prawn in half, lengthwise (save a few whole ones for garnish). Pick whitest stalks of celery; clean thoroughly. Cut in ⅛-inch-thick slices; combine with prawns and refrigerate overnight. Dress with Green Goddess Dressing to barely coat (about 1 cup). Pile lightly into a shallow salad bowl lined with large leaves of iceberg lettuce. Garnish with whole prawns and parsley sprigs; serve additional dressing on the side. Makes 16 servings.

GREEN GODDESS DRESSING:
2 cups mayonnaise
1 cup white wine vinegar
1 small can (2 oz.) rolled anchovies
with capers
½ cup chopped fresh parsley
1 small onion, finely chopped
(about ½ cup)
2 teaspoons dried tarragon leaves
½ teaspoon salt
1 cup whipping cream

Place mayonnaise, ¾ cup of the vinegar, drained anchovies, parsley, onion, tarragon, and salt into a blender; whirl until thoroughly blended. Combine remaining vinegar with cream and add to first mixture. Whirl again. Store in refrigerator until needed. Makes 4 cups dressing.

Shrimp with Lemon Dressing

The canned shrimp on this platter regains its fresh-caught flavor with an ice-cube chilling and a few hours' marinating in a lemony dressing.

Drain 1 can (4½ oz.) large shrimp; rinse in cold water. Chill in bowl of ice cubes and water 15 minutes; drain. Add shrimp to dressing made of 2 tablespoons tart French dressing, 1 tablespoon lemon juice, 1 teaspoon soy, 3 drops Tabasco. Chill. Mix shrimp and dressing with ⅓ cup finely sliced celery, serve on crisp water cress. Makes 1 serving as a main-dish salad.

Shrimp and Pineapple Tostado with Ham Sauce

½ pound cleaned, cooked small shrimp

Garlic French dressing

4 corn tortillas

Fat for frying

1½ cups diced cooked ham

1 tablespoon melted butter

1½ cups commercial sour cream

4 cups shredded lettuce

1 cup chopped water cress

¼ cup garlic French dressing

½ cup crumbled blue cheese

8 slices bacon, cooked until crisp, and crumbled

12 wedges fresh pineapple (or 12 spears canned pineapple)

Water cress, green pepper rings, lime wedges for garnish

Marinate shrimp in French dressing. In hot deep fat or shallow fat fry each tortilla until very crisp. Center on serving plates; keep warm. Lightly brown diced ham in melted butter. Add sour cream, and heat gently. Toss lettuce and water cress with the ¼ cup garlic French dressing. Spoon hot sour cream and ham sauce over tortillas. Arrange lettuce in stacks over the sour cream sauce, and in a bed encircling each tortilla. Drain shrimp; arrange over lettuce and water cress stacks. Sprinkle with blue cheese and bacon. Arrange pineapple wedges around tortillas. Garnish plates with water cress sprigs, green pepper rings, and lime wedges. Makes 4 tostados.

Tuna, Banana, Pineapple Salad

3 ripe bananas

1 cup drained diced pineapple

¼ cup sliced celery

¼ teaspoon salt

¾ cup salad dressing

2 tablespoons lemon juice

1 can (7 oz.) tuna, flaked

Lettuce

If you wish to serve a "conversation piece," here's a salad that fits into that category. The combination is unusual— and a pleasant taste surprise.

Peel and dice bananas and combine with diced pineapple. Mix celery, salt, salad dressing, and lemon juice. Fold in fruit, then add drained flaked tuna. Serve on crisp lettuce. Makes 6 to 8 servings.

Tuna-Nut Salad

1 package (10 oz.) frozen cut
green beans
2 cups shredded cabbage
3 tablespoons chopped chives or
green onions
1 large dill pickle, chopped
½ cup chopped walnuts
½ cup mayonnaise
1 tablespoon light cream
1 teaspoon lemon juice
½ teaspoon salt
1 small can (3½ oz.)
solid pack tuna
2 or 3 hard-cooked eggs, sliced
Lettuce
Minced parsley (optional)

Prepare green beans as directed on package, cooking them until just tender, but still slightly crisp; drain and chill. Combine the beans with cabbage, chives or onions, dill pickle, and walnuts; toss. Mix the mayonnaise with cream, lemon juice, and salt. Mix lightly into salad. Drain tuna, break into large pieces and add to salad with 2 of the sliced eggs. Toss very gently. Arrange in a lettuce-lined bowl or on individual plates. Garnish with hard-cooked egg slices and sprinkle with parsley, if you wish. Makes 6 servings.

Tuna Salad Niçoise

A tuna salad that makes a fine luncheon dish or first course at dinner is called Niçoise because it originated in Nice. Slice 1 head of lettuce and arrange it in a large shallow bowl. On it, in a symmetrical design, arrange 4 small peeled and quartered tomatoes, 1 cup cooked green beans, 1 cup diced, cooked potatoes, 1 red onion, sliced thin and the slices halved, 2 sliced hard-cooked eggs, and 1 can (7 oz.) solid-pack tuna. Garnish with 6 or 8 anchovy fillets and some Italian-style black olives. Just before serving, pour over French dressing. Makes 6 to 8 servings.

West Coast Salad

This salad introduces delicious bacon flavor in a crisp tuna salad.

1 large or 2 medium-sized
heads romaine
3 shallots, finely minced
1 can (7 oz.) tuna, flaked
2 hard-cooked eggs, chopped
6 slices bacon
2 tablespoons vinegar
Pepper

Wash, dry, and chill romaine; break into pieces in a large bowl. Add shallots, tuna, and eggs. Cook bacon until crisp; drain and break into bowl, reserving fat. Add vinegar and a few grindings of pepper to bacon fat in same pan. Heat and pour over salad, mixing gently. Taste, and add salt if necessary. Makes 6 servings.

Tuna-Stuffed Peppers

4 tablespoons fine dry bread crumbs
3 tablespoons tarragon vinegar
1 tablespoon capers, drained
¼ teaspoon garlic salt
4 tablespoons mayonnaise
1 can (7 oz.) tuna, flaked
2 large or 3 medium green peppers
2 tablespoons water
Greens

This tuna-filled pepper is seasoned with capers and served with lemon-seasoned mayonnaise.

Combine the bread crumbs with the vinegar, capers, garlic salt, mayonnaise, and tuna. Cut the green peppers in half, and remove the seeds and veins. Fill the pepper halves with the tuna mixture and arrange them in a casserole or baking dish. Add the 2 tablespoons water to the bottom of the casserole. Bake in a moderate oven (350°) for 45 to 50 minutes, or until the peppers are tender but still hold their shape. Chill until serving time. Serve on a bed of salad greens with lemon mayonnaise. Makes 4 to 6 servings as a salad accompaniment, 2 to 3 as a main course.

LEMON MAYONNAISE: Add 3 tablespoons lemon juice to ½ cup mayonnaise.

Crunchy Tuna Salad

1 can (7 oz.) tuna, flaked
½ cup finely chopped onion
3 tablespoons finely chopped green pepper
3 tablespoons chopped ripe olives
2 tablespoons chopped pimiento
½ cup mayonnaise
1 teaspoon garlic vinegar
1 tablespoon light cream
1 can (3 oz.) crisp Chinese noodles
Crisp greens for garnish

Chinese noodles are responsible for the crunchiness of this salad. They go in at the last minute so they stay crisp. Garnish each serving with two deviled egg halves, if desired.

Combine tuna, onion, green pepper, olives, and pimiento. Blend together the mayonnaise, vinegar, and cream until smooth; pour over tuna mixture and mix well. Chill. When ready to serve, add crisp noodles and mix lightly. Line a chop plate or 6 salad plates with greens; spoon on tuna salad. Makes 6 servings.

Tuna Appetizer Salad

On individual plates arrange a little curly endive (chicory) or shredded lettuce. On this put a thick slice of peeled tomato. Top each tomato with half a hard-cooked egg, round side up, and cover all with this tuna mayonnaise: 1 cup mayonnaise combined with ½ cup grated tuna, and 1 teaspoon lemon juice. Enough for 6 to 8 servings. Garnish each plate with ripe olives if you wish.

EGGS, CHEESE, RICE & PASTE SALADS

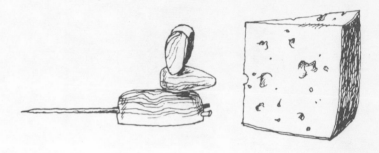

Eggs, Cheese, Rice

and paste salads can be main dishes or accompaniments. They are especially good choices for barbecue menus as most of them can be prepared well in advance—many of them actually improve when they are chilled for a while so flavors have a chance to blend. They also stand up well if they have to wait a bit while the entrée is being served.

Most of these salads are hearty. They can replace an oven-baked casserole as an accompaniment to a main dish —and you'll note that we have suggested serving several of them in lettuce-lined casseroles for a pleasing change from the usual salad bowl.

Feature one of these salads in your next picnic menu— they are perfect replacements for the usual potato salad. Try them, too, for warm-weather meals, with cold meats, a fresh-baked hot bread (your own recipe or a "quickie" mix), and a refreshing beverage. Almost any one of the salads in this chapter can stand alone as a main dish for a luncheon.

Garnishes are important here, for often salads in this group are not colorful in themselves. A wedge of bright red tomato, a sprig of deep green water cress, or a ring of golden pineapple will add a touch of color as well as a good flavor note of its own.

Curried Rice Salad

2 cups chilled, cooked rice
1 medium-sized green pepper,
shredded
2 tablespoons drained pimientos,
cut in strips
2 tablespoons raisins
2 tablespoons chopped parsley
2 tablespoons chopped green onion
½ cup olive oil
⅓ cup wine vinegar
1 tablespoon lemon juice
1 clove garlic, minced or mashed
1 tablespoon sugar
½ teaspoon curry powder
Salt and pepper to taste
Salad greens
Green pepper rings
Tomato wedges

An ideal accompaniment for barbecued lamb or barbecued or fried chicken.

Using two forks, toss together the rice, green pepper, pimientos, raisins, parsley, and onion. Chill thoroughly.

Combine oil, vinegar, lemon juice, garlic, sugar, curry powder, salt, and pepper. Just before serving, pour over salad and toss thoroughly.

Arrange salad in a bowl or casserole. Garnish with crisp greens, green pepper rings, and tomato wedges. Makes 4 servings.

Cracked Wheat Salad

Mix together 2 cups cooked cracked wheat or bulghour with ½ cup Italian style dressing. Chill at least 30 minutes. Toss with about 1 quart bite-size pieces iceberg lettuce. Season to taste with salt and freshly ground pepper. Makes 6 servings.

Ham and Cheese Rice Salad

1 package (10 oz.) frozen peas
1⅓ cups boiling salted water
1⅓ cups packaged pre-cooked rice
¾ cup mayonnaise
½ cup chopped dill pickle
1 teaspoon grated onion
Lettuce
1 cup slivered Swiss cheese
1 cup slivered cooked ham
Tomato slices

This salad has some of the heartiness of an oven-baked casserole dish, but you serve it crisp and cold. It can stand alone as a main dish luncheon or supper salad.

Add peas to the boiling water; cover and cook until water boils again. Stir in rice. Cover, remove from heat, and let stand 10 minutes. With a fork, mix in mayonnaise, dill pickle, and grated onion. Chill thoroughly. At serving time, arrange in individual casseroles edged with crisp lettuce, or pile into a lettuce-lined bowl. Top salads with slivers of Swiss cheese and ham. Garnish with tomato slices. Offer additional mayonnaise. Makes 4 to 6 servings.

Year-Around Salad

1 medium-sized head of lettuce
2 bananas
3 hard-cooked eggs
1 tablespoon vinegar
½ teaspoon sugar
¾ teaspoon salt
2 tablespoons mayonnaise

Shred lettuce, slice bananas, and coarsely chop eggs. Toss together with the vinegar, sugar, salt, and mayonnaise. Serve at once. Makes 4 servings.

Double Cheese Salad

2 cups (1 pound) creamed cottage cheese
½ cup crumbled Roquefort or blue cheese
1 cup crumbled crisp bacon (½ pound)
2 tablespoons sliced stuffed olives
2 tablespoons mayonnaise
Lettuce or chicory

Crumbled, crisp bacon—a whole cup of it—turns cottage cheese and Roquefort or blue cheese into a hearty salad with a decisive flavor.

Blend the cottage cheese with the Roquefort or blue cheese, crisp bacon, olives, and mayonnaise; chill for 1 hour. Serve on crisp lettuce or chicory. Serves 6.

Western Patio Salad

½ cup vinegar
½ cup water
½ cup sugar
1 teaspoon dry mustard
2 tablespoons flour
¼ teaspoon each paprika and celery salt
¼ teaspoon salt
2 eggs, separated
1 tablespoon butter or margarine
½ cup light cream
2 cups uncooked salad macaroni

Bring vinegar and water to boiling point. Mix the sugar, mustard, flour, paprika, celery salt, salt, and beaten egg yolks together and stir into vinegar and water. Cook until thick. Remove from heat, add butter, and fold in stiffly beaten egg whites and cream. Cook macaroni as usual in plenty of boiling salted water; drain, blanch, and mix with hot dressing. Chill salad and serve with a garnish of pimiento or quartered tomatoes. Makes 6 servings.

Onion and Cheese Salad

1 large sweet onion
¼ pound Swiss cheese
¼ pound cooked ham
1 large green pepper
3 tablespoons wine vinegar
⅓ cup salad oil (part olive oil,
    if desired)
Salt and freshly ground
    pepper to taste
Lettuce

Slice onion very thin, cut slices in half, separate rings, and cover with ice water. Chill for about 2 hours. Cut into matchlike pieces Swiss cheese, ham, and green pepper; combine with drained onion. Stir in vinegar, salad oil, salt, and pepper. Chill. Serve on lettuce. Makes 6 servings.

Stuffed Pimiento Salad

2 cups cooked macaroni
½ cup crushed pineapple, drained
1 medium-sized tomato, diced
½ teaspoon salt
Dash of pepper
2 teaspoons prepared mustard
3 tablespoons commercial
    sour cream
4 teaspoons wine vinegar
1 teaspoon scraped onion
2 jars or cans (4 oz. each)
    whole pimientos
Lettuce

Bright red pimientos hold a fruit-flavored macaroni salad. This is good with cold slices of turkey or fried chicken.

Combine the cooked macaroni with the drained pineapple, tomato, salt, and pepper. Mix together the mustard, sour cream, wine vinegar, and onion. Toss this dressing with the macaroni mixture. Drain the whole pimientos and stuff each with the macaroni salad. Serve on a bed of lettuce; surround with green onions if you wish. Makes 4 to 6 servings.

Orange-Wheat Salad

1 cup quick-cooking cracked wheat
    or bulghour
2 tablespoons butter
2 cups water
¼ cup mayonnaise
Juice of 1 lemon
Juice of 1 orange
2 teaspoons chopped chives
1 teaspoon sugar
1 teaspoon salt
1 can (11 oz.) mandarin oranges,
    drained

Brown quick-cooking wheat in the butter in a large saucepan. Add 2 cups water, bring to a boil, cover, and simmer 15 minutes. Remove lid to let steam escape so the cooked wheat will dry a bit.

When cracked wheat is cool, toss to prevent kernels from sticking together, and place in refrigerator until you're ready to add dressing.

Make dressing by mixing together the mayonnaise, lemon juice, orange juice, chives, sugar, and salt. Toss with chilled wheat and orange sections. You might save a few orange sections for a garnish. Makes 4 to 6 servings.

Barbecue Salad Bowl

1 jar (2 oz.) stuffed
green olives
1 cup mayonnaise
¼ cup wine vinegar
2 teaspoons sugar
1 teaspoon chili powder
Pinch of cayenne
½ teaspoon salt
¼ teaspoon pepper
½ package (14 oz.) shell macaroni,
cooked and drained
1 can (1 lb.) garbanzos
1 can (7 oz.) tuna, flaked
½ cup raisins (optional)
1 dill pickle, chopped
6 green onions, sliced
½ cup chopped parsley
1 clove garlic, minced or mashed
Crisp greens
2 tablespoons capers

Paste salads take many forms, but we think this is a most unusual one. The raisins add sweetness to the rather tart salad combination.

Drain liquid from olives (retain olives for use later), and combine with mayonnaise, vinegar, sugar, chili powder, cayenne, salt, and pepper. Toss dressing with macaroni, garbanzos, tuna, raisins, pickle, onions, parsley, and garlic. Heap into a salad bowl lined with crisp greens; garnish with halved stuffed olives and capers. Makes 8 servings.

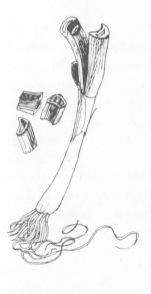

MOLDED &
FROZEN SALADS

Molded and Frozen

salads are, for the most part, quite simple to make; yet they present a very festive picture. Encasing salad ingredients in a shimmering, sparkling gelatin, or a creamy-smooth base, seems to give them a new personality. Even the simplest molded or frozen salad has a special party air about it—and these salads are favorites with hostesses because they can be prepared well ahead of time.

In deciding which molded or frozen salad to include in a meal, be guided by the general rules of menu harmony. The rich, mousse-type molded or frozen salad is hearty fare and should be served with simple dishes. Many salads in this chapter can be dessert salads. Spicy salads, in individual molds, are good meat accompaniments.

Salad molds are obtainable in varied sizes and shapes; and many other containers—such as freezer cartons, loaf pans, or muffin tins—make satisfactory molds. (To measure the capacity of a container, simply measure the amount of water needed to fill it.)

To unmold a salad, first loosen the mold by running the tip of knife around the edge of the salad. Then dip the mold quickly in warm water. Place a serving dish on top of the mold, and invert quickly. Remove the mold, and then arrange greens or garnishes, if desired.

Washington Apple Salad

¼ cup cinnamon-flavored candies

½ cup plus 2 tablespoons water

1 package (3 oz.) apple-
flavored gelatin

1 cup apple sauce

1 cup small curd cottage cheese,
forced through a fine wire strainer

1 cup diced unpeeled red apples

¾ cup finely chopped celery

⅓ cup chopped walnuts

2 tablespoons mayonnaise

½ cup ice cold evaporated milk

2 teaspoons lemon juice

Greens

To cut back on calories, cottage cheese and evaporated milk are used instead of the more typical cream cheese and whipping cream.

Boil together candies and water, stirring until candies are dissolved. Remove from heat; add gelatin and stir until dissolved. Blend in apple sauce and cottage cheese; chill until syrupy. Stir in apples, celery, walnuts, and mayonnaise. Combine evaporated milk and lemon juice and whip until stiff. Fold into gelatin mixture. Pour into a 2-quart mold and chill until set. Unmold on greens, and serve. Makes 6 servings.

Avocado Cheese Aspic

1 package (3 oz.) lime-flavored
gelatin

1½ cups hot water

2 packages (3 oz. each)
cream cheese

2 tablespoons light cream or milk

1 tablespoon lemon juice

1 teaspoon onion juice

1 teaspoon salt

Few drops each Worcestershire
and Tabasco

1 cup finely diced avocado

1 cup finely sliced celery

2 tablespoons finely
chopped pimiento

Lettuce

3 or 4 hard-cooked eggs, cut
in quarters lengthwise

This pale green molded salad flecked with bits of pimiento is an attractive addition to a party buffet or a luncheon. The base is a rather sweet blend of cream cheese and lime-flavored gelatin.

Dissolve gelatin in hot water and chill until syrupy. Blend together cream cheese, cream or milk, lemon juice, onion juice, salt, Worcestershire, and Tabasco. Add to dissolved gelatin and mix well. Fold in avocado, celery, and pimiento. Pour into a 1½-quart mold and chill until firm. Unmold on a bed of lettuce; border with egg quarters. Makes 10 servings.

Molded Guacamole Ring

2 envelopes (2 tablespoons)
unflavored gelatin
½ cup cold water
1½ cups boiling water
6 tablespoons lemon or lime juice
1½ teaspoons grated onion
2¼ teaspoons salt
Dash of Tabasco
3 cups mashed avocados,
(approximately 3 large avocados)
¾ cup mayonnaise

This salad, held together lightly by gelatin, tastes like a very good guacamole. Fill the ring with shrimp, crab, or chicken salad. To be at its best, it should be eaten the day it is made, for when it stands for any longer, it turns brown around the edges.

Soften gelatin in cold water and dissolve in boiling water. Add lemon or lime juice, onion, and seasonings. Peel and mash avocados. While gelatin mixture is still liquid, stir in avocado pulp. Fold in mayonnaise. Pour into 10-inch ring mold and chill until firm. Unmold and fill center with chilled seafood or chicken salad. Makes 8 servings.

Avocado and Tomato Salad Mold

AVOCADO ASPIC:
1 envelope (1 tablespoon)
unflavored gelatin
¼ cup cold water
1 cup boiling water
1 teaspoon sugar
2 tablespoons lemon juice
1 cup mashed avocado (1 large)
½ cup each commercial sour
cream and mayonnaise
1 teaspoon salt
Pepper and dash of cayenne

TOMATO ASPIC:
1 envelope (1 tablespoon)
unflavored gelatin
¼ cup cold water
1 cup boiling water
2 tablespoons sugar
1 can (10 oz.) tomato soup
1 tablespoon lemon juice
¼ teaspoon salt
Greens

You mold an avocado-sour cream aspic on top of a tomato aspic for this light green and red salad.

Soften gelatin in cold water, pour in boiling water, and stir until dissolved. Add sugar and 1 tablespoon of the lemon juice. Chill until slightly thickened. Immediately after mashing avocado, add the other tablespoon lemon juice, sour cream, mayonnaise, salt, pepper, and cayenne. Mix thoroughly with chilled gelatin. Pour into 2-quart mold. Chill until set.

Soften gelatin in cold water; dissolve in boiling water. Add sugar, soup, lemon juice, and salt. Pour over firm avocado aspic. Chill until set. Unmold on greens. Makes 8 to 10 servings.

Frozen Avocado Molds

1 cup sieved avocado pulp
3 tablespoons lime juice
3 tablespoons salad oil
½ teaspoon salt
2 tablespoons finely grated
Cheddar cheese
1 can (9 oz.) sliced pineapple
Lettuce

Mix thoroughly avocado pulp, lime juice, oil, salt, and cheese. Spoon into 4 molds and pat down with back of spoon. Freeze until firm. Arrange pineapple slices on lettuce. Dip molds in lukewarm water and turn out a frozen mold on each slice of pineapple. Makes 4 servings.

Cherry Salad

1 can (1 lb. 13 oz.) sweet dark
cherries (pitted if available)
⅓ cup lemon juice
Water
1 package (3 oz.) orange-flavored
gelatin
¾ cup coarsely chopped
pecan meats
1 bottle (3 oz.) pimiento-stuffed
green olives
Lettuce
Mayonnaise or sour cream dressing

Drain the syrup from the cherries into a pint measuring cup. Add the lemon juice and enough water to give you 1¾ cups of liquid. Turn into a saucepan, heat, pour over orange-flavored gelatin, and stir until the gelatin is completely dissolved. Let chill until syrupy.

While gelatin mixture is chilling, pit cherries (if unpitted). If you prefer very crisp nut meats, toast the pecan meats in a moderate oven for a few minutes. Drain the olives and cut in slices. When gelatin is ready, add the cherries, pecan meats, and olives. Turn into a 1½-quart mold or individual molds. Chill until firm. Unmold and garnish with butter lettuce or inside leaves of head lettuce. Serve with mayonnaise or a sour cream dressing. Makes 8 servings.

Melon Mold with Cherries

1 can (1 lb. 13 oz.) Bing cherries
1 can (1 lb. 4 oz.) pineapple tidbits
Water
1 package (3 oz.) lemon-flavored
gelatin
1 medium-sized cantaloupe
Fresh mint
Melon balls for garnish

Melon cubes go into the gelatin base of this molded salad, and melon balls garnish the salad after it is turned out of the mold.

Drain juice from cherries and pineapple tidbits; measure, and add enough water to make 1 cup of each. Dissolve lemon-flavored gelatin in the 1 cup of pineapple juice. Stir in cherry juice; chill until syrupy. Half, seed, and peel cantaloupe, and cut into small cubes. Place melon cubes in bottom of a 1½-quart ring mold. Add pineapple and cherries to chilled gelatin; pour over melon cubes. Chill until firm. Unmold on bed of fresh mint and garnish with melon balls. Makes 8 servings.

Cranberry and Orange Relish Salad

1½ pounds (6 cups) raw cranberries
3 cups sugar
4 envelopes (4 tablespoons) unflavored gelatin
1 cup orange juice
2 cups chopped celery
¾ cup chopped walnut meats
Endive
Mayonnaise (optional)

This tart, crisp, molded salad can replace the usual cranberry relish as an accompaniment to roast turkey.

Grind cranberries, using a fine blade; mix in sugar and let stand about 15 minutes, stirring occasionally. Meanwhile, soften gelatin in orange juice; stir over hot water until dissolved. Combine cranberry and orange mixtures, add celery and walnut meats. Pour into 12 individual molds (8 oz. size). Chill until set, preferably overnight. Unmold salads on curly endive on individual salad plates. Serve with mayonnaise if desired. Makes 12 servings.

Molded Grape Salad

2 cups grapes (Tokay, preferably)
¾ cup French dressing
1 cup hot water
1 package (3 oz.) lemon-flavored gelatin
½ cup orange juice
¼ cup lemon juice
½ teaspoon finely chopped onion
¼ teaspoon salt
1 small package (3 oz.) cream cheese
Lettuce

Wash grapes, slit, and seed. (Reserve 12 grape halves.) Marinate in French dressing 30 minutes; drain. Save dressing for later use. Pour hot water over gelatin and stir until dissolved. Stir in orange juice, lemon juice, onion, and salt. Chill until gelatin mixture mounds slightly when dropped from a spoon. Stir in marinated grapes. Spoon into 6 individual molds or a 1-quart mold; chill until set. Soften cheese and form into 6 balls. Place each ball between 2 of the remaining grape halves. Unmold salad on lettuce, and garnish with cheese balls. A mixture of half mayonnaise, half whipped cream may be served as a dressing. Makes 6 servings.

Gingered Grape and Pear Mold

1 cup hot water
1 package (3 oz.) apple-flavored gelatin
1 cup ginger ale
1 cup diced fresh pears
½ cup halved Thompson seedless grapes
¼ cup chopped pecan meats (toasted, if desired)
2 teaspoons finely chopped candied ginger
Greens
Mayonnaise or other salad dressing

Ginger ale and candied ginger add a special spiciness to this amber-colored gelatin fruit salad.

Pour hot water over flavored gelatin in a bowl, and stir until dissolved; cool. Stir in ginger ale and chill until syrupy. Mix together the pears, grapes, nut meats, and ginger, and stir into the gelatin mixture; turn into a 1-quart ring mold or 6 individual molds. Chill until firm. Unmold on greens. Serve with a bowl of mayonnaise in the center of the ring. Makes 6 servings.

Jellied Melon Salad

1 tablespoon (1 envelope)
unflavored gelatin
¼ cup cold water
2 tablespoons lemon juice
1¼ cups ginger ale
4 cups small cantaloupe
balls or cubes
2 cups small watermelon
balls or cubes
6 or 8 rings (about 1 inch thick)
honeydew melon

FRUIT-CHEESE DRESSING:
¾ cup creamed cottage cheese
1½ tablespoons lemon juice
¼ cup orange juice
1 teaspoon each lemon peel and
orange peel
2 tablespoons honey

This tangy, colorful melon salad has a low-calorie dressing.

Soften the gelatin in cold water; stir over hot water until thoroughly dissolved. Add the lemon juice and ginger ale; stir until well blended. Combine the cantaloupe and watermelon and arrange in the bottom of 6 or 8 individual salad molds or a 2-quart salad mold or square baking pan. Pour the gelatin mixture over melon balls. Chill until firm. Unmold or cut in squares; arrange each serving on a melon ring. To make the dressing, combine all ingredients and whirl smooth in electric blender; or press cottage cheese through strainer and whip with remaining ingredients. Makes 6 to 8 servings.

Mandarin Orange Salad Mold with Fruited Cream

2 packages (3 oz. each)
lemon-flavored gelatin
1 cup hot water
1 cup cold water
2 tablespoons lemon juice
1 can (12 oz.) frozen orange
juice concentrate, undiluted
2 cans (11 oz. each) mandarin
oranges, drained

DRESSING:
1 banana
1 can (9 oz.) crushed
pineapple, well drained
1 cup mayonnaise
½ pint (1 cup) whipping cream
Endive

Concentrated orange juice brings an emphatic tang and golden color to this gelatin salad. The dressing of puréed banana, crushed pineapple, and whipped cream doubles the fruit flavor.

Dissolve gelatin in the hot water. Stir in cold water, lemon juice, undiluted orange juice, and the mandarin oranges. Turn into a 1½-quart salad mold and let chill until firm. For the dressing mash the banana and mix with the crushed pineapple and mayonnaise. Whip cream until stiff, and fold in. Turn into a sauce bowl. Unmold salad on a bed of crisp endive or other greens, and pass the dressing separately. Makes about 8 servings.

Lime-Lemon-Orange Layered Salad

This unusual combination of fruits and vegetables has a sour cream layer in the center.

FIRST LAYER:
1 package (3 oz.) lime-flavored gelatin
2 cups hot water
2 carrots, coarsely grated (1 cup)
3 stalks celery, finely sliced (⅔ cup)
1 medium-sized avocado, cubed (1 cup)

Dissolve lime-flavored gelatin in water; chill until it is syrupy, then fold in carrots, celery. and avocado. Turn into two 4 by 12-inch loaf pans or one 9 by 14-inch baking dish. Chill until firm.

SECOND LAYER:
1 package (3 oz.) lemon-flavored gelatin
1 cup hot water
½ pint (1 cup) commercial sour cream
2 bananas

Prepare lemon-flavored gelatin, using only 1 cup hot water. Cool. Stir in sour cream, blending well. Slice bananas and fold in. Turn out over the firm lime gelatin layer, and chill until firm.

THIRD LAYER:
1 can (1 lb. 13 oz.) apricot halves or 1 cup cooked fresh or dried apricot halves
Water
2 packages (3 oz. each) orange-flavored gelatin
2 cups cold water
1½ cups seedless grapes
Greens

Drain juice from apricots and measure juice; add enough water to make 2 cups liquid. Heat to boiling, add orange-flavored gelatin, and stir until dissolved; stir in 2 cups cold water. Chill until syrupy. Stir in washed grapes and 1 cup of the apricot halves. Turn out over the sour cream layer, and chill overnight.

Turn out on a platter lined with crisp salad greens. Makes 16 servings.

Papaya-Sour Cream Mold

1 package lemon-flavored gelatin
1 can (12 oz.) papaya juice
1 tablespoon lemon juice
1 can (11 oz.) mandarin orange sections
1 can (1 lb.) seedless grapes
½ pint (1 cup) commercial sour cream

Papaya juice is the base for this molded salad. It includes juicy mandarin orange segments and seedless grapes. When seedless grapes are in season, substitute 1 cup of fresh grapes for the drained canned grapes.

Dissolve lemon-flavored gelatin in hot papaya juice; stir in lemon juice; chill until syrupy. Drain liquid from both the mandarin orange sections and the seedless grapes (save the liquid for punch or other molded salads). Fold the sour cream and the drained fruits into the gelatin mixture, turn into 6 molds, and chill until firm. Makes 6 servings.

Molded Persimmon Salad

1 package (3 oz.)
lemon-flavored gelatin
1½ cups hot water
3 medium-sized ripe persimmons
Water cress or crisp greens
Sour cream or mayonnaise
Slivered almonds, if desired

Dissolve gelatin in hot water. Chill until syrupy. Peel persimmons and force pulp through a sieve. Blend pulp with gelatin mixture and pour into 5 or 6 individual molds or a 1½-pint mold. Chill until firm. Dip molds quickly in warm water and unmold on water cress. Serve with sour cream or mayonnaise, topped with almonds, if desired. Makes 5 or 6 servings.

PINEAPPLE VARIATION:
Drain and save syrup from 1 can (8 oz.) crushed pineapple. Add enough water to make 1½ cups. Bring to a boil. Proceed as directed above, adding crushed pineapple along with persimmon pulp to gelatin mixture.

Orange-Pineapple-Apricot Salad Ring

FIRST LAYER:
1 package (3 oz.)
orange-flavored gelatin
2 cups hot water

This tart, fruit-filled salad is especially eye-catching.

Dissolve orange-flavored gelatin in hot water; pour into a 3-quart ring mold, and chill until firm.

SECOND LAYER:
2 envelopes (2 tablespoons)
unflavored gelatin
6 tablespoons lemon juice
1 can (1 lb. 4 oz.) crushed pineapple
½ teaspoon salt
1½ large packages cream cheese
1 cup mayonnaise
2 teaspoons horse-radish
1 cup finely sliced celery
½ pint (1 cup) whipping cream

Soften 2 envelopes unflavored gelatin in lemon juice. Drain juice from the pineapple, and add enough water to make 1½ cups; heat to boiling, and add softened gelatin; stir until dissolved. Stir in salt. Chill until syrupy. Cream the cream cheese until light, and beat in the mayonnaise and horse-radish; blend into the chilled pineapple-flavored gelatin. Fold in crushed pineapple and celery. Whip cream until stiff, and fold in. Spread over orange layer and chill until firm.

THIRD LAYER:
2 envelopes (2 tablespoons)
unflavored gelatin
¼ cup cold water
1 can (1 lb. 13 oz.) apricot halves
Juice of 1 lemon
(3 tablespoons juice)
Juice of 2 oranges (⅔ cup juice)
1 cup blanched almonds,
finely chopped

Soften 2 envelopes unflavored gelatin in cold water. Drain juice from apricots, and add enough water to make 1½ cups; heat to boiling, add softened gelatin, and stir until dissolved. Stir in lemon juice and orange juice. Chill until syrupy. Chop apricots and stir in. Add chopped almonds. Carefully spoon over the firm pineapple layer. Let chill overnight. Turn out on a platter lined with greens. Makes 16 servings.

Double Decker Pineapple-Cherry Salad

Sandwiched between this double decker fruit mold is a thin layer of cream cheese. Olives contrast pleasingly with the juicy sweet cherries and bits of pineapple.

FIRST LAYER:

1 can (1 lb. 4 oz.) sliced pineapple
Water
1 package (3 oz.) cherry-flavored gelatin

Drain pineapple; add enough water to the syrup to make 1¾ cups liquid. Heat liquid to boiling; dissolve cherry-flavored gelatin in the hot liquid; chill until syrupy. Cut pineapple slices into ¼-inch pieces and stir into the gelatin mixture. Turn into an 8-inch-square pan. Let chill until the gelatin layer is firm.

SECOND LAYER:

1 package (3 oz.) cream cheese
2 tablespoons light cream

Let cream cheese warm to room temperature; mix it with the light cream until light and fluffy; spread over the gelatin, and chill until firm.

THIRD LAYER:

1 can (1 lb.) pitted Bing cherries
⅓ cup lemon juice
Water
1 package (3 oz.) orange-flavored gelatin
½ cup sliced stuffed olives

Drain cherries. Add lemon juice to cherry syrup and then enough water to make 1¾ cups liquid; heat to boiling, add orange-flavored gelatin, and stir until dissolved. Chill until syrupy. Add cherries and sliced olives, and pour over the cream cheese mixture. Chill overnight. Unmold on a bed of crisp greens. Serves 8 to 10.

Pineapple, Kumquat, and Pomegranate Salad

¼ cup sherry or port wine
2 cups diced fresh pineapple
1 cup pomegranate seeds
½ cup seeded and thinly sliced preserved kumquats
1 package (3 oz.) cream cheese
2 tablespoons each kumquat syrup and lemon juice
¼ teaspoon seasoned salt
¾ teaspoon dry mustard
3 tablespoons sugar
1½ cups whipping cream

Pour sherry or port over pineapple, pomegranate seeds, and kumquats. Meanwhile, blend cream cheese with kumquat syrup, lemon juice, seasoned salt, dry mustard, and sugar. Add cream and whip until stiff. Fold in fruit and wine. Turn into two 1-quart refrigerator trays and freeze until firm. Cut and serve on greens or from a chilled pineapple shell. Makes 8 to 10 servings.

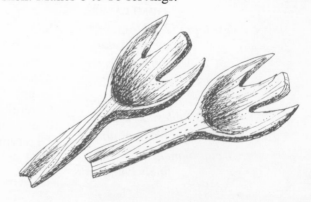

Blueberry Salad Mold

1¼ cups fresh, canned, or
frozen blueberries
1 cup water or blueberry juice
2 tablespoons cornstarch
Pinch of salt
⅛ teaspoon nutmeg
¼ teaspoon cinnamon
¼ cup sugar
1 package (3 oz.) lemon-
flavored gelatin

Combine blueberries with liquid and bring to a boil. Mix together cornstarch, salt, spices, and sugar. Add to blueberries gradually, and cook until thick. Prepare lemon gelatin as directed on package. Pour half of the gelatin into a mold and let it get firm. Mix the remaining gelatin into the blueberry mixture and pour on the top of the firm gelatin. Allow several hours for setting. Makes 6 to 8 servings.

Molded Strawberry Ring

1 package (3 oz.) strawberry-
flavored gelatin
2 cups hot water
2 packages (3 oz. each)
cream cheese
3 tablespoons light cream
½ teaspoon salt
½ cup finely chopped nut meats
1 pint strawberries

A festive dinner salad: whole fresh strawberries and nut-filled cream cheese balls in a shimmering strawberry gelatin mold. For an extra garnish, fill the center of the ring mold with pineapple sherbet.

Dissolve flavored gelatin in hot water. Pour a thin layer of the gelatin into the bottom of a 1½-quart ring mold or loaf pan; chill until set. Chill remaining gelatin mixture until syrupy. Meanwhile, blend cheese, cream, salt, and nut meats; form into 12 balls. Wash and hull berries; select the largest berries to place inside ring mold. Alternate berries and cheese balls in mold. Carefully pour remaining gelatin over berries and cheese, and chill for several hours, or until set. Unmold on chop plate and garnish with remaining berries. Makes 8 servings.

Strawberry-Blueberry Mold

3¾ cups water
2 packages (3 oz. each) wild
cherry or cherry-flavored gelatin
¼ cup pale dry sherry
1 basket strawberries
(approximately 1 pint)
1 package frozen blueberries,
practically thawed
2 cans (1 lb. each) seedless grapes
Greens
French dressing

Heat 2 cups of the water, add flavored gelatin, and stir until dissolved. Stir in the remaining 1¾ cups water and the wine; chill until syrupy. Wash and halve strawberries, and arrange in the bottom of a 3-quart ring mold, or use individual molds. Pour in enough of the chilled gelatin to cover berries; chill. Mix the remaining gelatin with blueberries and grapes, and pour into mold. Chill until firm. When ready to serve, unmold on greens that have been tossed in French dressing. Makes 10 to 12 servings.

Artichoke Ring

6 to 8 cooked artichokes
1 envelope (1 tablespoon) unflavored gelatin
¼ cup cold water
½ cup boiling water
¼ cup lemon juice
Garlic to taste
½ teaspoon salt
¼ teaspoon paprika
½ cup whipping cream
1 cup mayonnaise

For more flavor, add a clove of garlic to the water in which you cook the artichokes for this molded salad. Strips of pimiento crisscrossed over the artichoke ring make it even more attractive.

Scrape all the tender meat from the artichoke leaves and cut the hearts into quarters. Soften gelatin in cold water; dissolve in boiling water; add lemon juice and seasonings; cool until slightly thickened. Whip cream and fold into gelatin mixture along with mayonnaise and artichoke pulp and hearts. Pour into an 8-inch ring mold and chill until firm. Fill the center with cooked, chilled vegetables, tomato quarters, or avocado and shrimp marinated in French dressing. Makes 8 to 10 servings.

Beet and Olive Salad

2 packages (3 oz. each) lemon-flavored gelatin
1 cup hot water
1 cup cold water
1 can (1 lb.) julienne-style beets
12 pimiento-stuffed green olives chopped
½ cup chopped sweet pickles
1 tablespoon each onion salt and garlic salt
Lettuce
French dressing

This is spicy, with chopped sweet pickles and pimiento-stuffed green olives.

Dissolve gelatin in hot water; stir in cold water. Drain beets; add drained liquid to dissolved gelatin. Chill until syrupy. Blend in beets, olives, and pickles; season with onion salt and garlic salt. Pour into an 8-inch-square pan or individual molds. Chill until firm. Unmold salad on lettuce and serve with French dressing. Makes 8 to 10 servings.

Borsch Jellied Salad

1 can (10½ oz.) consommé
Water
1 package (3 oz.) lemon-flavored gelatin
1½ tablespoons vinegar
⅔ cup drained julienne-style beets
1 cup finely shredded cabbage
1 tablespoon grated onion
1 teaspoon salt
Dash of pepper
Lettuce
Sour cream dressing

Crisp cabbage and firm beets give an interesting texture to this consommé-flavored gelatin salad.

Heat consommé and enough water to make 2 cups liquid. Pour liquid over gelatin and stir until dissolved. Add vinegar. Chill until syrupy. Stir beets, cabbage, onion, salt, and pepper into chilled gelatin. Turn mixture into an 8-inch-square pan. Chill until firm. Unmold salad on shredded lettuce; top with dressing. Makes 6 to 8 servings.

Molded Gazpacho Salad

1 envelope (1 tablespoon)
unflavored gelatin
About 1½ cups tomato juice
1 large ripe tomato
2 tablespoons vinegar or pickle juice
⅛ teaspoon crushed garlic
1 medium-sized cucumber, chopped
1 peeled and seeded green chili,
chopped
¼ cup chopped onion
¾ teaspoon salt
⅛ teaspoon freshly ground pepper
Greens

The ingredients usually used in the Spanish cold soup, *gazpacho,* are used here in a molded salad. It makes a very nice summer meal with cold cuts and hot rolls.

Soften the gelatin in ¼ cup of the tomato juice for about 5 minutes. Meanwhile heat 1 cup of the tomato juice; add the gelatin and stir until thoroughly dissolved. Chop the fresh tomato, saving the juice; add vinegar and remaining tomato juice to make ½ cup liquid. Add to the hot mixture with the garlic, cucumber, green chili, onion, salt and pepper. Pour into a 1-quart mold. Chill until firm. Unmold on a bed of crisp greens. Makes 4 to 6 servings.

Tomato Fruit Jelly

1¾ cups tomato juice
1 package (3 oz.) raspberry-
flavored gelatin
1 tablespoon sugar
¼ teaspoon salt
2 tablespoons cider vinegar
or lemon juice
½ cup chopped cucumber
½ cup chopped celery
¼ cup minced green onion
Mayonnaise or sour cream dressing
Greens

Bring one cup of the tomato juice to a boil. Add the gelatin, and stir until thoroughly dissolved. Add the remaining ¾ cup cold tomato juice, sugar, salt, and vinegar or lemon juice. Chill until the mixture begins to thicken. Stir in the cucumber, celery, and green onion. Turn into a 1-quart mold or into 4 or 5 individual molds. Chill until firm. Unmold and serve with mayonnaise or sour cream dressing. Garnish the salad plates with crisp greens. Makes 4 or 5 servings.

Molded Baked Bean Salad

1 package (3 oz.) lemon-
flavored gelatin
1 cup boiling water
½ cup catsup
3 tablespoons tarragon vinegar
2 teaspoons horse-radish
¼ teaspoon Tabasco
2 cups canned baked beans
2 tablespoons each chopped green
onion and dill pickle
½ cup sliced celery
Lettuce
French dressing

A jellied, baked bean salad rates as a novelty in the category of molded salads. In this one, crisp onion, pickle, and celery provide a contrast to the soft beans.

Dissolve the gelatin in boiling water; add catsup, vinegar, horse-radish, and Tabasco; chill until syrupy. Mix in beans, onion, pickle, and celery, and pour into loaf pan, 1-quart ring mold, or 8 individual molds. Chill until set. Turn out of mold onto lettuce, and serve with a sharp French dressing to which a few capers may be added. Makes 8 servings.

Potato Salad Roll

4 cups cubed cooked potatoes
½ cup finely sliced celery
½ cup finely chopped sweet pickle
2 tablespoons finely chopped parsley
2 tablespoons finely chopped pimiento
4 hard-cooked eggs, chopped
1 tablespoon grated onion
¾ teaspoon salt
1 tablespoon lemon juice
¾ cup mayonnaise or salad dressing
Relishes for garnish (optional)

When well chilled, this salad roll slices neatly. Frost the top with mayonnaise, and garnish with pimiento and parsley, if you wish to dress it up a little.

Toss together the potatoes, celery, sweet pickle, parsley, pimiento, and hard-cooked eggs. Add the onion, salt, lemon juice, and mayonnaise; mix thoroughly. Turn salad out onto a large piece of aluminum foil and shape into a roll, approximately 8 by 4 by 2½ inches. Roll up in foil. Chill 24 hours. Turn out on a platter and garnish with radish roses, pitted ripe olives, and tomato wedges, if desired. Cut in slices to serve. Makes 8 servings.

Ham and Tongue Aspic

ASPIC:
3 cans (10½ oz. each) consommé
1 cup water
1 medium-sized onion, sliced
2 stalks celery, sliced
2 envelopes (2 tablespoons) unflavored gelatin
½ cup water

Bring to a boil the consommé and the 1 cup water. Add onion and celery. Cover and simmer 15 minutes. Strain and save liquid. To hot consommé add gelatin that has been softened in the ½ cup water; stir until dissolved. Pour into a 1½ or 2-quart mold, and set mold in ice water that is just a little deeper than the top level of gelatin mixture. Let stand until a layer of aspic about ¼ inch thick has coated sides of mold. Pour out liquid center and save.

FILLING:
Hard-cooked egg slices
Cooked beef tongue slices
1½ cups diced, cooked ham
2 hard-cooked eggs, diced
⅔ cup chopped celery
1 green onion, minced
2 tablespoons finely chopped pimiento
Butter lettuce
Mayonnaise
Prepared mustard

Decorate aspic shell with slices of hard-cooked egg, dipped first in aspic, then attached to sides and bottom; let chill until eggs hold securely. Pour a little of the aspic (if it gets thick, set in hot water and stir) into mold, and line with slices of cooked beef tongue. Let chill while you combine with remaining aspic the ham, diced hard-cooked eggs, celery, onion, and pimiento. Fill mold and chill at least 4 hours or overnight. Unmold on butter lettuce. Cut and serve with a dressing of mayonnaise flavored to taste with prepared mustard. Makes 8 to 10 servings.

Turkey Mousse

1 envelope (1 tablespoon)
unflavored gelatin
¼ cup cold water
1½ cups well-seasoned turkey or
chicken stock or 2 chicken
bouillon cubes dissolved in
1½ cups hot water
2 cups diced, cooked turkey
½ cup sliced celery
½ cup cooked peas
½ cup mayonnaise
¼ cup each chopped pimiento,
pickle relish, and slivered
blanched almonds
Crisp salad greens

This molded salad is almost a complete meal because it contains a large amount of turkey, celery, and peas. It is a colorful salad to feature at a buffet supper. Or if you wish to serve it as the main course for Sunday supper, accompany it with hot tomato soup and plenty of corn sticks.

Soften gelatin in cold water. Heat turkey stock, add gelatin, and stir until it dissolves. Chill until syrupy, then fold in the turkey meat, celery, peas, mayonnaise, pimiento, pickle relish, and almonds. Turn into a 2-quart mold; chill until firm, at least 3 to 4 hours. Unmold on a platter and garnish with crisp greens before serving. Makes 8 servings.

Cream of Chicken Mousse

1 can (10½ oz.) cream of
chicken soup
1 can of water
2 envelopes (2 tablespoons)
unflavored gelatin
¾ cup cold water
⅓ cup mayonnaise
½ cup heavy cream, whipped
1 can (6 oz.) minced chicken or
turkey or ¾ cup leftover fowl
⅓ cup sliced, stuffed olives (2 oz. jar)
1 large stalk celery, thinly sliced
1 tablespoon lemon juice
¼ teaspoon salt
Paprika to taste
Lettuce
Parsley

Pour soup into pan, fill can with water, and blend into soup until smooth. Heat to the boiling point. Soften gelatin in cold water and stir into soup. Cool until it begins to thicken. Mix in mayonnaise and blend thoroughly. Fold in whipped cream. Add remaining ingredients. Chill in 8 individual molds. When set, unmold on lettuce and garnish with parsley. If dressing is desired, thin mayonnaise with tarragon vinegar, or use a tart French dressing. Makes 8 servings.

Curry Ring with Chicken Salad

1½ envelopes (1½ tablespoons)
unflavored gelatin

½ cup dry white table wine

2 cups chicken broth (use stock
from cooking chicken for salad,
canned broth, or chicken stock
base dissolved in water)

2 teaspoons curry powder

1 cup mayonnaise

1 tablespoon finely chopped
green onion

1 cup finely sliced celery

1 finely chopped pimiento

1 teaspoon salt

3 hard-cooked eggs, chopped

⅔ cup sliced ripe olives (or ⅓ cup
each sliced ripe olives and stuffed
green olives)

Crisp greens

CHICKEN SALAD:

3 cups diced, cooked chicken

1 cup finely sliced celery

1 tablespoon grated onion

1 tablespoon lemon juice

½ teaspoon salt

Dash of cayenne

½ cup mayonnaise

½ cup slivered salted almonds

1 cup fresh pineapple pieces
(optional)

This luncheon salad can be prepared a day in advance for an easy buffet meal to serve to a large group. You fill the center of the ring mold with a festive salad of chicken, celery, fresh pineapple, and salted almonds.

Soften gelatin in cold wine. Heat 1 cup of the chicken broth with the curry powder to the boiling point; add gelatin and stir until dissolved. Stir in 1 cup cold stock and chill until syrupy. Fold in mayonnaise; then mix in green onion, celery, pimiento, salt, hard-cooked eggs, and olives. Turn into an oiled 1½-quart ring mold or 8 individual ring molds; chill until firm.

Unmold ring mold on a bed of greens and fill the center of the ring with the chicken salad. Makes 8 generous servings.

Toss together the diced chicken, celery, onion, lemon juice, salt, and cayenne. Chill several hours. When ready to serve, blend in mayonnaise, almonds, and pineapple.

Molded Shrimp Salad

1 tablespoon (1 envelope)
unflavored gelatin
¾ cup water
1½ cups yogurt
½ cup tomato catsup
½ teaspoon salt
¼ teaspoon dill weed
2 cups diced cooked shrimp
Cucumber slices

Yogurt is the creamy base for this rich tasting shrimp salad.

Soften gelatin in ¼ cup of the water; add remaining ½ cup water, heated to boiling, and stir to dissolve. Blend in yogurt, catsup, salt, and dill weed. Chill until syrupy. Stir in shrimp and pour mixture into a 2-quart mold. Chill until set, about 3 hours. Unmold on serving dish and garnish with cucumber slices. Makes 6 to 8 servings.

Frosted Salmon Mousse

1 can (1 lb.) red salmon
1 envelope (1 tablespoon)
unflavored gelatin
¼ cup cold water
¼ cup boiling water
½ teaspoon salt
2 tablespoons each lemon juice
and vinegar
1 tablespoon sugar
2 teaspoons grated onion
1 teaspoon horse-radish
⅓ cup sliced ripe olives
¼ cup finely sliced celery
½ cup mayonnaise

Remove skin and bones from salmon. In a medium-sized bowl, soften gelatin in cold water; add boiling water and stir until dissolved. Mix in salt, lemon juice, vinegar, sugar, grated onion, and horse-radish. Cool until slightly thickened. Stir in flaked salmon, olives, celery, and mayonnaise. Turn into a 5 by 9-inch loaf pan and chill until firm. Turn out on a platter and frost with avocado spread.

AVOCADO SPREAD:
Combine ½ cup sieved avocado, ⅔ cup sour cream, ⅔ teaspoon salt, and a dash of cayenne. Frost top of salmon loaf; serve remainder of avocado spread separately.

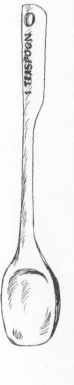

Molded Sardine Ring

1 envelope (1 tablespoon)
unflavored gelatin
1½ cups water
2 bouillon cubes
2 teaspoons lemon juice
1 teaspoon onion juice
3 hard-cooked eggs
2 cans (3¼ oz. each) sardines,
drained and boned
Tomato wedges, chopped parsley
for garnish

Soften gelatin in ¼ cup of water. Heat remaining 1¼ cups water to boiling, add bouillon cubes, lemon juice, onion juice, and softened gelatin, stir until bouillon cubes and gelatin are dissolved. Pour ¼ of the gelatin mixture into a 1-quart ring mold and chill until set. Thinly slice eggs and arrange around ring mold on chilled gelatin. Break sardines into short lengths and place over the eggs. Carefully spoon in remaining aspic mixture. Chill until firm. Unmold and garnish with tomato wedges dipped in chopped parsley. Makes 6 servings.

Whole Salmon in Aspic

1 whole salmon, about 8 pounds
Salt to taste
½ cup water
⅓ to ½ pound white-fleshed fish
1 small onion, sliced
1 sprig parsley
1 stalk celery
2½ cups water
1 teaspoon salt
Dash white pepper
4 teaspoons lemon juice
1 envelope (1 tablespoon)
unflavored gelatin
½ cup cold water
Pimiento strips or green pepper
rings, sliced ripe or stuffed
green olives

If the head is removed from the salmon, leave the collar intact. Sprinkle inside of fish with salt. Place fish on sheet of heavy foil, cup the edges, then pour in the ½ cup water so the salmon will steam as it cooks. Wrap foil over fish, then fold and crimp edges of foil together. Place in a shallow pan and bake in a moderate oven (350°) for 30 minutes or until fish will flake easily when tested with a fork. While fish is still warm, fold back foil and carefully pull off skin. Place salmon in refrigerator to chill thoroughly.

To make the aspic, combine the white fish with onion, parsley, celery, and 2½ cups water; cover and simmer gently for 25 minutes. Strain through a fine wire strainer, and measure 1½ cups of the fish stock. Add salt, pepper, and lemon juice. Meanwhile soften gelatin in the ½ cup cold water. Bring stock to a boil, and stir in gelatin until dissolved.

Transfer the cold salmon to a serving platter and pour over a thin layer of aspic; put back in refrigerator until aspic sets. Decorate fish with strips of pimiento or green pepper rings, and sliced ripe or green olives, dipping them into the syrupy aspic so they will stick to the fish. Pour another coat of aspic over fish and decorations. Refrigerate until decorations set in place. You might check once or twice to see that the decorations haven't slipped. Makes 12 to 15 servings.

Molded Tuna and Cabbage Salad

¾ cup hot water
1 package (3 oz.)
lime-flavored gelatin
½ cup cold water
2 tablespoons vinegar
2 tablespoons lemon juice
½ teaspoon salt
1 can (7 oz.) tuna, flaked
1 cup shredded cabbage
¼ cup (4 tablespoons) chopped
dill pickle
3 hard-cooked eggs, sliced
Crisp greens for garnish

Lime-flavored gelatin makes a colorful wrapping for layers of tuna, cabbage, pickle, and hard-cooked eggs.

Pour hot water over flavored gelatin and stir until dissolved; stir in cold water, vinegar, lemon juice, and salt; chill until syrupy. Arrange flaked tuna in the bottom of a 1½-quart ring mold or loaf pan; pour one-half of the cooled gelatin into the mold; chill until firm. In the following order, arrange over the firm gelatin two layers each of the cabbage, dill pickle, and hard-cooked egg slices, pour over the remaining half of the gelatin mixture. Chill until firm, about 2 hours. Unmold on greens. Makes 6 servings.

Lemon-Lime Tuna Mold

1 package (3 oz.) lemon-flavored gelatin
1 package (3 oz.) lime-flavored gelatin
2 cups hot water
2 cups cold water
2 teaspoons prepared mustard
2 teaspoons lemon juice
⅔ cup mayonnaise
¾ cup sliced celery
1 cup cooked peas
1 tablespoon finely chopped onion
2 tablespoons chopped pimiento
2 hard-cooked eggs, coarsely chopped
2 cans (7 oz. each) flaked tuna
Lettuce, radishes, and ripe olives for garnish

Green peas, pimiento, and chopped hard-cooked eggs are colorful spots in this pale green tuna mold. Prepared mustard and lemon juice add enough sharpness to the gelatin base to keep it from being sweet.

Combine flavored gelatins in a large bowl; pour in hot water, and stir until gelatin is dissolved. Stir in cold water; chill until syrupy. Combine the mustard, lemon juice, and mayonnaise; stir into gelatin. Fold in the celery, peas, onion, pimiento, hard-cooked eggs, and flaked tuna. Turn mixture into a 2½-quart ring mold. Chill for 3 hours, or until firm. To serve, unmold on lettuce and garnish with radishes and a few ripe olives. Makes 12 servings.

Crab Mousse

¾ to 1 pound crab meat, flaked
¼ cup (4 tablespoons) lemon juice
1 tablespoon sherry
1 envelope (1 tablespoon) unflavored gelatin
¼ cup cold water
1 cup sliced celery
3 tablespoons chopped green pepper
1 tablespoon chopped pimiento
10 stuffed green olives, chopped
2 hard-cooked eggs, chopped
1 teaspoon salt
¼ teaspoon freshly ground pepper
½ pint (1 cup) whipping cream
Greens

Fresh crab meat marinated in lemon juice and sherry adds a tang to this salad.

Mix crab meat with lemon juice and sherry and let stand. Soften gelatin in cold water and dissolve over boiling water. Stir dissolved gelatin into crab meat and lemon. Add celery, green pepper, pimiento, olives, eggs, salt, and pepper. Whip cream and fold in. Spoon into 1½-quart ring mold and chill 3 hours, or until firm. Unmold on bed of greens and fill center of ring with pickles or a tossed green salad with a sharp dressing. Makes 6 to 8 servings.

Crab Meat Salad Mold

2 envelopes (2 tablespoons)
unflavored gelatin
½ cup cold water
1 cup chili sauce or catsup
1 cup whipping cream
1 cup mayonnaise
1 to 2 tablespoons lemon juice
1½ cups fresh or canned crab meat
½ cup grated American cheese

Soften gelatin in cold water for 5 minutes. Heat chili sauce or catsup in double boiler. Add softened gelatin and stir until dissolved. Remove from heat and cool. Whip cream; fold into mayonnaise, and then stir in the chili sauce mixture. Add lemon juice to taste. Stir in crab and grated cheese. Pour into a 2-quart ring mold and chill until firm. May be served with or without salad dressing. Makes 8 to 10 servings.

Molded Avocado Ring with Seafood Salad

1 cup boiling water
1 package (3 oz.) lemon-
flavored gelatin
1 cup mayonnaise
1 tablespoon lemon juice
1 teaspoon salt
1 large avocado
½ pint (1 cup) whipping cream
Chicory

SEAFOOD SALAD:

1½ cups grapefruit segments
2 cups crab meat or small shrimp
1 cup sliced celery
2 tablespoons lemon juice
⅓ cup French dressing
½ teaspoon celery salt

Dungeness crab and grapefruit go in the center of this pale green avocado ring.

Pour boiling water over the flavored gelatin, stirring until dissolved. Cool until syrupy. Stir in the mayonnaise, lemon juice, and salt. Peel and sieve avocado (should have 1 cup sieved pulp) and stir in. Whip cream until thick, but not stiff, and fold in. Turn into a 1-quart ring mold and chill until firm. Unmold on greens. Toss together lightly the grapefruit segments, crab meat, celery, lemon juice, French dressing, and celery salt. Fill center of ring with seafood salad. Makes 8 servings.

Molded Cheese Salad

1 envelope (1 tablespoon)
unflavored gelatin
¼ cup cold water
1 can (9 oz.) crushed pineapple
1 pound (4 cups) ground
Cheddar cheese
½ cup chopped walnut meats
1 cup mayonnaise
1 cup (½ pint) whipping cream

Use a small square of this salad as the center of interest for a fruit plate. Surround it with pears and orange and grapefruit segments on a bed of romaine.

Soften gelatin in water. Heat the pineapple, add gelatin, and stir until dissolved; cool. Mix in the cheese (which has been run through the medium blade of the food chopper), nut meats, mayonnaise, and the cream which has been beaten until it peaks. Turn into a deep 8 by 12-inch baking pan or two loaf pans, each 5 by 9 inches. Chill until set; cut in squares or slice to serve. Makes 10 to 12 servings.

Three-Cheese Salad Mold

2 envelopes (2 tablespoons)
unflavored gelatin
½ cup cold water
1 cup hot water
¼ teaspoon salt
¼ teaspoon paprika
2 tablespoons lemon juice
1 large package (8 oz.) cream cheese
4 tablespoons (¼ cup) Roquefort
or blue cheese
⅔ cup milk
4 tablespoons (¼ cup) grated
American cheese
½ green pepper, seeded and chopped
2 tablespoons chopped pimiento
1 tablespoon finely minced onion
(optional)
1 cup (½ pint) whipping cream
Lettuce, tomato wedges, cucumber
sticks for garnish

The smooth texture of this salad comes from cream cheese; the flavor accents are Roquefort and American cheese.

Soften gelatin in cold water; pour over hot water and stir until gelatin is dissolved; add salt, paprika, and lemon juice; cool. Mash cream cheese with the Roquefort or blue cheese until mixture is blended but still slightly lumpy. (If you prefer a more subtle Roquefort cheese flavor, beat mixture until smooth.) Add milk and stir until well mixed; stir in grated American cheese and cooled gelatin, along with green pepper, pimiento, and onion.

Whip cream until thick but not stiff; fold into cheese and gelatin mixture; turn into a 1½-quart ring mold and chill until firm, about 2 hours. To serve, unmold on crisp lettuce and garnish with tomato wedges and cucumber sticks. Makes 6 to 8 servings.

Mustard Ring

4 eggs
¾ cup sugar
1 envelope (1 tablespoon)
unflavored gelatin
1½ tablespoons dry mustard
½ teaspoon turmeric
¼ teaspoon salt
1 cup water
½ cup cider vinegar
½ pint (1 cup) whipping cream
Greens

Here is an excellent salad-relish accompaniment for ham because it is sweet, tart, colorful, and spicy, as well as attractive. For contrast to the smooth texture of the mustard-flavored ring mold, fill the center with a cabbage slaw.

Beat eggs in top of double boiler. Mix together thoroughly the sugar and unflavored gelatin; stir in mustard, turmeric, and salt. Add the water and vinegar to the eggs, stir in the sugar mixture, and cook over boiling water until slightly thickened, stirring continuously. Cool until it is thick. Whip cream and fold in. Turn into a 1½-quart ring mold. When firm, unmold and, if desired, fill center with cole slaw to which you might add frozen or canned pineapple chunks or diced winter pears. Garnish with chicory, cress, or other feathery greens. Makes 8 servings.

Sieved Egg-Green Onion Salad Ring

2 envelopes (2 tablespoons)
unflavored gelatin
1 cup cold water
9 hard-cooked eggs
1 cup mayonnaise
7 green onions, finely sliced
1¼ teaspoons salt
Pepper to taste
¾ teaspoon Worcestershire
½ teaspoon paprika
½ teaspoon garlic salt
1 teaspoon prepared mustard
½ cup sliced radishes
Salad greens
Thousand Island dressing

For a colorful luncheon salad, you might mound cooked shrimp or crab meat in the center of this egg salad ring.

Sprinkle gelatin in cold water to soften; place over boiling water and stir until dissolved; cool. Put the eggs through a sieve or a ricer; mix in mayonnaise, green onions, salt, pepper, Worcestershire, paprika, garlic salt, mustard, and radishes. Combine the egg mixture with the cooled gelatin, and turn into a greased 1½-quart ring mold. Chill until set. Unmold on greens. Serve Thousand Island dressing. Makes 8 servings.

Mincemeat Salad Ring

1 envelope (1 tablespoon)
unflavored gelatin
¼ cup cold water
1 package (9 oz.) dry mincemeat
2 cups chilled ginger ale
¼ cup lemon juice
⅓ cup chopped nut meats
Sour cream or whipped cream
Grated lemon peel

Unusually sweet for a gelatin salad, this mincemeat ring is very good with cold sliced ham or turkey.

Sprinkle gelatin into cold water; let stand 5 minutes. Break up mincemeat into saucepan, and add 1 cup of the ginger ale. Bring to a boil, stirring constantly; boil 1 minute. Remove from heat, and stir in gelatin mixture, lemon juice, and nut meats; stir until gelatin is dissolved. Cool. Stir in remaining 1 cup ginger ale. Turn into 1½-quart ring mold; chill at least 2 hours. To serve, unmold and top with sour cream or whipped cream sprinkled with a little grated lemon peel. Makes 8 servings.

SALAD
DRESSINGS

A Salad Dressing

gives the final flavor balance to a salad. It should point up and blend the flavors of the salad ingredients. Most vegetables, meats, seafood, and eggs need a piquant dressing to set off their delicate flavors to best advantage; on the other hand, tart fruits take kindly to the addition of a creamy, sweet dressing. A salad of crisp greens or simple lettuce wedges must have an outstanding dressing to give it character.

There is no one "compulsory" dressing for any one salad; it is a matter of individual tastes, and variety is the key to good eating.

The salad dressing may accent the entrée. Horse-radish may be used in the salad dressing when you serve roast beef, baked ham, or smoked tongue. A combination of greens tossed with a dressing seasoned with Parmesan or blue cheese goes well with spaghetti, enchiladas, or any of the spicy Italian and Mexican dishes.

Wait until the last possible moment to add dressing to a salad, and then use just enough dressing to accent the salad. When dressing is added to a tossed green salad, there should be just enough to coat all the leaves; you should not end up with a pool of dressing at the bottom of the salad bowl.

Standard French Dressing

1 teaspoon salt
⅛ teaspoon pepper
⅛ teaspoon paprika
¼ cup vinegar
¾ cup salad oil

Mix the dry ingredients with the vinegar, add the oil, and beat or shake well before using. Wine vinegar, tarragon, malt, or cider vinegar may be used, or any combination of these; or lemon or grapefruit juice may replace the vinegar. Additional seasonings, such as Worcestershire sauce, onion, and garlic, may be added. Makes about 1 cup dressing.

Tomato French Dressing

½ cup sugar
2 teaspoons salt
1½ teaspoons dry mustard
½ teaspoon paprika
1 can (10½ oz.) condensed tomato soup
1 cup salad oil
¾ cup cider vinegar
¼ cup tarragon vinegar
1 teaspoon Worcestershire
1 medium-sized onion, grated
1 clove garlic, grated or left whole (optional)

Combine ingredients and beat well until the sugar is dissolved and the mixture is thick and rich. Makes about 3 cups dressing. (This will keep indefinitely in the refrigerator.)

Tangy French Dressing

1 teaspoon salt
Dash of cayenne
¼ teaspoon pepper
½ teaspoon dry mustard
1 teaspoon Worcestershire
1 tablespoon (or more) finely minced onion
1 clove garlic, finely minced
2 tablespoons vinegar
6 tablespoons salad oil

Combine all ingredients in a bowl; beat hard with a rotary or electric beater until well blended. If dressing is not used at once, be sure to beat or shake again just before serving. Makes about ½ cup dressing.

Sweet-Sour Fruit Salad Dressing

1 egg
1 teaspoon salt
1 tablespoon flour
5 teaspoons sugar
¼ cup (4 tablespoons) vinegar
¼ cup (4 tablespoons) water
1 small can (6 oz.) evaporated milk

The sweet-sour flavor of this salad dressing is a good contrast to the mildness of melons, peaches, and pears. For variety, add ½ teaspoon grated orange peel.

Beat egg together with salt, flour, and sugar in top of a double boiler; stir in vinegar and water. Stirring constantly, cook over boiling water until smooth and slightly thick. Remove from heat and beat in evaporated milk. Store in refrigerator until ready to use. Makes 1 cup.

Vinaigrette Dressing

2 hard-cooked egg yolks
¼ cup malt vinegar
6 tablespoons salad oil
2 green onions chopped fine
Salt and coarse black
pepper to taste

Mash yolks to a paste with vinegar; gradually blend in oil; add remaining ingredients and mix well. Serve with cold asparagus or broccoli, or with salad greens. Makes about ¾ cup dressing.

Celery Seed Salad Dressing

½ cup sugar
1 teaspoon salt
½ teaspoon dry mustard
1 teaspoon onion juice
¼ cup cider vinegar
1 cup salad oil
1 to 1½ teaspoons celery seeds
1 teaspoon paprika

This tart dressing is delicious on fresh or canned fruit, cole slaw, or a combination of fruit and cabbage.

Combine sugar, salt, mustard, onion juice, vinegar, salad oil, celery seeds, and paprika in a small bowl and beat well. Chill well before serving. Makes 1¼ cups dressing.

Papaya Seed Dressing

1 cup sugar
1 teaspoon salt
1 teaspoon dry mustard
1 cup wine vinegar
2 cups salad oil
1 small onion
1 tablespoon papaya seeds

Serve this dressing on fruit salads, such as the fruit plate of papaya, orange, banana, and pineapple slices pictured on page 148.

Mix sugar, salt, mustard, and vinegar. Add oil gradually, beating constantly. Grate onion; add along with papaya seeds; stir to blend well. If dressing separates on standing, whip it up again before serving. Makes 3 cups dressing.

Piquant Dressing

1 cup salad oil
⅓ cup wine vinegar
¼ cup dry white table wine
1½ teaspoons Worcestershire
3 or 4 drops Tabasco
1 tablespoon brown sugar
1½ teaspoons salt
1 teaspoon paprika
¼ teaspoon coarse black pepper
1 clove garlic, peeled

This light dressing goes well with most green salads. It's our first choice for the Green Salad, Smörgåsbord Style, page 14.

Combine all the ingredients in a covered pint jar. Shake until very well blended. Set aside several hours or overnight before using. Discard garlic. Makes 1½ cups.

Low Calorie Dressing

1 cup cider vinegar
2 tablespoons catsup
2 tablespoons brown sugar
1 tablespoon chili sauce
⅓ cup water
½ teaspoon liquid garlic
½ teaspoon dry mustard
¼ teaspoon each paprika and
    black pepper
⅛ teaspoon salt

There is no oil in this salad dressing, so it should have special appeal for weight watchers.

Place all ingredients in a bowl or jar, and beat or shake well. Makes about 2 cups dressing.

Chili Sauce Salad Dressing

⅔ cup sugar
1 teaspoon each salt, celery seed,
    and paprika
½ teaspoon pepper
1 green pepper, seeded and
    finely chopped
1 pimiento, finely chopped
1 medium-sized onion, grated
Juice of 2 lemons (⅓ cup juice)
¾ cup vinegar
1½ cups salad oil
1 bottle (12 oz.) chili sauce

You can toss this pimiento and green pepper-flecked salad dressing with many types of salad ingredients—mixed greens, mixed vegetables, crab, or shrimp.

In a 1½-quart jar with a tight-fitting cover, put the sugar, salt, celery seed, paprika, and pepper. Add the green pepper, pimiento, onion, lemon juice, vinegar, oil, and chili sauce; cover jar tightly and shake well. Refrigerate. Makes 1 quart dressing.

Caesar Style Dressing

¾ cup salad oil
3 tablespoons lime or lemon juice
⅓ cup grated Parmesan cheese
2 tablespoons finely chopped green onion
1 teaspoon salt
¾ teaspoon dry mustard
½ teaspoon garlic salt
¼ teaspoon coarse black pepper
½ teaspoon Worcestershire or soy

This is a modified Caesar dressing; you can make it up early to toss with broken romaine leaves. It contains no raw egg, yet retains the characteristic flavor of true Caesar dressing. It has a particularly good clinging quality; bits of cheese nestle in the dips of the leaves.

Combine all ingredients in a covered jar and shake thoroughly; chill. Shake again before using. Makes 1½ cups dressing.

Minced Vegetable Salad Dressing

1 medium-sized onion
1 can (4 oz.) pimientos
1 large green pepper
1 cup salad oil
¾ cup sugar
1 tablespoon salt
¾ cup vinegar

Use this colorful dressing on wedges of lettuce or over a salad of mixed raw and cooked vegetables.

Run the onion, pimientos, and seeded green pepper through the medium blade of the food chopper. Put ground vegetables in a quart jar. Add oil, sugar, salt, and vinegar. Shake well. Store in the refrigerator. Shake again each time you use it. Makes 1 quart of dressing.

Roquefort French Dressing

Combine ¼ cup crumbled Roquefort cheese and ½ cup French dressing; shake or stir well before serving. Serve with vegetable or green salads.

Barbara Worth Salad Dressing

1 large clove garlic
2 teaspoons salt
1 cup olive oil or salad oil
½ cup red wine vinegar
½ cup heavy cream
1 tablespoon sesame seeds
Freshly ground black pepper to taste

Dice garlic on a chopping board; sprinkle with salt, then work salt and garlic together, using the flat blade of a table knife, until garlic is completely blended with salt. Combine with remaining ingredients; stir well or shake in a jar. Allow dressing to ripen for several hours, and stir or shake well just before using. Makes 4 cups dressing.

Poppy Seed French Dressing

¾ cup sugar
1 teaspoon dry mustard
1 teaspoon salt
⅓ cup cider vinegar
1 cup salad oil
1 tablespoon very finely
    minced onion
1 teaspoon each poppy seeds
    and sesame seeds

This sweet French dressing with crunchy black poppy seeds and nut-flavored sesame seeds is ideal to serve over all kinds of fruit salads. Sesame seeds have a more nut-like flavor if you toast them first. Stir or shake the seeds as they brown.

Sift sugar, mustard, and salt together into a bowl. Blend in vinegar. With a rotary beater, gradually beat in oil. Stir in onion, poppy seeds, and sesame seeds. Chill thoroughly in a quart jar. Shake well before serving over any fruit salad. Makes 1½ cups dressing.

Mayonnaise

2 egg yolks
1 teaspoon salt
1 teaspoon sugar (optional)
1 teaspoon dry mustard
Dash of cayenne
2 to 4 tablespoons lemon juice
    or vinegar
2 cups salad oil

In a deep bowl, thoroughly mix the egg yolks with salt, sugar, mustard, and cayenne. Stir in 2 tablespoons lemon juice or vinegar. While beating briskly with a rotary beater, start adding the oil, a few drops at a time. Beat well after each addition until about ½ cup of the oil has been added. Beat in the remaining oil, adding it about 2 tablespoons at a time. Makes about 1 pint dressing.

Thousand Island Dressing

1 cup mayonnaise
3 tablespoons chili sauce
1 tablespoon chopped sweet pickle
2 tablespoons chopped stuffed olives
1 hard-cooked egg, chopped fine
½ teaspoon grated onion
½ cup whipped cream or ¼ cup
    French dressing

Mix ingredients in the order given and chill thoroughly before serving. Serve with vegetable salads.

Russian Dressing

To 1 cup mayonnaise, add 2 tablespoons each chili sauce and finely chopped pimiento or green pepper, and ½ teaspoon each vinegar and paprika. Mix well. Half a hard-cooked egg, chopped fine, and 1 tablespoon chopped chives may also be added. Delicious with green, vegetable, egg, or seafood salads.

Caviar Mayonnaise

Gently mix together 1 cup mayonnaise, 3 to 4 tablespoons red caviar, 1 tablespoon lemon juice, and 1 teaspoon grated onion. Use in place of plain mayonnaise with any seafood salad, or toss with chilled, crisp salad greens. If necessary, thin the dressing with a little cream so that it will mingle more readily with the greens. You might also use this as a dip for prawns, crab legs, potato chips, or raw vegetables.

Water Cress Salad Dressing

½ bunch water cress
1 clove garlic, minced or mashed
1 cup mayonnaise
Salt to taste
2 teaspoons lemon juice

In this mayonnaise dressing, water cress provides a spicy flavor and a bright green color. For a time-saver, put all ingredients in your blender and blend just until water cress is finely minced.

Chop water cress and garlic very fine. Stir into mayonnaise; add salt to taste and lemon juice. Chill. Serve over wedges of head lettuce or over a salad of orange and grapefruit segments. Makes 1½ cups of dressing.

Cucumber Salad Dressing

½ cup shredded cucumber, drained
¾ cup mayonnaise
¼ teaspoon herb blend for salad
2 green onions, finely minced
2 teaspoons red wine vinegar
⅛ teaspoon basil
¼ teaspoon salt

Mix cucumber with mayonnaise. Stir in remaining ingredients and chill until ready to serve. Makes about 1½ cups dressing.

Honey Lime Dressing

Juice of 2 large fresh limes
2 tablespoons light, mild honey
¾ cup salad oil
⅛ teaspoon salt

Honey sweetens this salad dressing made with lime juice. It is particularly good on a fruit, melon, or lettuce salad. It's best to make up only a small quantity of this dressing at one time so the lime doesn't lose its fresh flavor.

Strain lime juice and blend in honey. Add oil and salt and pour into a jar or covered plastic container. Shake well. Store in refrigerator. Shake again before using.

Fruit Salad Dressing

1 can (6 oz.) frozen orange juice
1 can (6 oz.) frozen pineapple juice
Pinch of salt
1 tablespoon maraschino cherry juice
3 tablespoons honey
1 tablespoon cornstarch
¼ teaspoon celery seeds
¼ teaspoon dried parsley

The tartness of both the concentrated orange and the pineapple juice makes this an ideal dressing for both fresh and canned fruits. For a richer dressing, blend in an equal amount of whipped cream.

Blend the undiluted orange and pineapple juices with salt, cherry juice, honey, and cornstarch in top of double boiler. Cook over hot water until thickened. Stir in the celery seeds and parsley, and chill. Makes about 1 cup dressing. Toss with desired fruits, or serve separately.

Creamy Banana Dressing

2 medium-sized ripe bananas
⅓ cup mayonnaise
⅓ cup buttermilk
3 tablespoons lemon juice
2 teaspoons prepared horse-radish
½ teaspoon salt
1 teaspoon sugar
¼ teaspoon Tabasco

Here's a delicious dressing for cabbage slaw, especially those combinations that include fruit. Try it on a salad made of finely shredded cabbage with seeded grapes and a few chopped nuts.

Using a blender, whip together bananas, mayonnaise, buttermilk, lemon juice, horse-radish, salt, sugar, and Tabasco. If you don't have a blender, use your electric mixer to beat the ingredients together until smooth. Makes 1⅔ cups dressing.

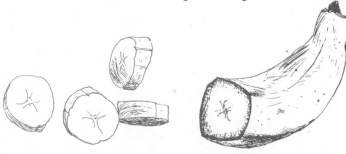

Creamy Dressing for Molded Salads

2 eggs
½ cup honey
Juice of 1 lime or lemon
½ pint (1 cup) whipping cream

A fluffy, not too sweet, dressing that is best with molded fruit or dessert salads. It should be served the same day it is made. The type of honey used will determine the flavor of the dressing.

Beat eggs until light, stir in honey and lemon or lime juice. Cook over boiling water until thick; cool. Whip cream until stiff and fold into honey mixture. Chill at least 1 hour before serving. Makes enough for 8 salads.

Sour Cream Dressing

½ cup sugar
3 teaspoons salt
¼ teaspoon white pepper
2 teaspoons prepared mustard
3 tablespoons flour
2 cups (1 pint) commercial
sour cream
¾ cup strained lemon juice
¼ cup water
Whipped cream

You may serve this dressing either cold or hot. When you use it cold with shredded cabbage or fruit, thin it with whipped cream. When you wish it hot, simply reheat and mix immediately with potatoes, cabbage, or garden greens.

Blend sugar, salt, pepper, mustard, and flour together in the top of a double boiler; gradually add sour cream, stirring constantly; combine lemon juice and water and pour in. Cook over boiling water, stirring constantly, until thick and smooth. Remove from heat; stir occasionally while cooling to prevent a film from forming. Store in a covered container in the refrigerator. Thin with whipped cream to desired consistency before serving. Makes 3 cups dressing.

Anchovy Sour Cream Salad Dressing

3 hard-cooked eggs
1 bunch green onions
1 clove garlic
1 can (2 oz.) anchovies
2 tablespoons mayonnaise
1 tablespoon vinegar
½ pint (1 cup) commercial
sour cream
Few drops of Tabasco

Finely chop hard-cooked eggs, green onions (tops and all), garlic, and anchovies. Stir in mayonnaise, vinegar, sour cream, and Tabasco. Anchovies supply the salt. Chill for several hours before using on fish or vegetable salads.

Date Sour Cream Dressing

1 package (7 oz.) pitted dates
½ cup water
1 half-pint (1 cup) commercial
sour cream

Combine this creamy sweet dressing with sliced fresh fruits or crisp chopped apples and celery for a salad of surprising character.

Bring dates and water to a boil and simmer 10 minutes. Cool. Chop dates very fine. Blend dates and sour cream thoroughly with a fork or rotary beater. Makes 1⅔ cups dressing.

Marshmallow Dressing

12 marshmallows
1 egg
1 tablespoon vinegar
1 tablespoon sugar
1 teaspoon salt
1 cup (½ pint) whipping cream

Dissolve marshmallows by heating in the top of double boiler over hot water, stirring occasionally. Beat egg, stir in vinegar, sugar, and salt; add to marshmallows. Cook 2 minutes, or until mixture thickens, stirring constantly. Cool. Whip cream and fold into cold mixture. Serve over fruit or molded salads. Makes enough for 8 salads.

Cottage Cheese Salad Dressing

½ pint (1 cup) large curd
cottage cheese
3 tablespoons French dressing
3 tablespoons vinegar
1 tablespoon grated
Parmesan cheese
¼ teaspoon garlic purée or
1 clove garlic, mashed
¼ teaspoon each salt and pepper

The base of this low-calorie dressing is cottage cheese. Garlic and Parmesan cheese make it pungent.

In a mixing bowl, combine the cottage cheese, French dressing, vinegar, Parmesan cheese, garlic, salt, and pepper, and beat with a rotary beater until smooth and creamy. Makes 1½ cups dressing.

Mint Cream Dressing

½ cup large curd cottage cheese
1 tablespoon mint-flavored jelly
Grated peel and juice of 1 lime
¼ cup fresh orange juice

Whirl cottage cheese, jelly, lime peel, lime juice, and orange juice in a blender until smooth; or force through a fine wire strainer several times. Spoon over your favorite sliced fruits. Makes ¾ cup dressing.

Apricot Cream Dressing

1 small package (3 oz.) cream cheese
½ cup apricot nectar
1 tablespoon lemon juice
¼ cup mayonnaise
Dash of salt

Apricot nectar gives this cream cheese dressing a tangy flavor. Serve it with a fruit plate that includes a variety of fruits.

Soften cream cheese with a fork; blend in apricot nectar and beat until smooth. Add the lemon juice, mayonnaise, and salt, and mix well. Makes about 1 cup dressing.

Creamy Cheese-Avocado Dressing

1 medium-sized ripe avocado
⅓ cup commercial sour cream
2 tablespoons finely minced
green onion
1 tablespoon lime or lemon juice
½ teaspoon each salt, garlic salt,
and Worcestershire
⅓ cup crumbled Roquefort cheese
¾ cup salad oil
¼ cup each dry white table wine
and wine vinegar

Peel and remove seed from avocado; mash fruit until very smooth. Blend in sour cream, onion, lime juice, salt, garlic salt, and Worcestershire. Mash cheese until almost smooth; blend in oil, wine, and vinegar. Combine with avocado mixture. Chill well. Makes about 3 cups dressing.

Roquefort Cheese Dressing

About 1 pint (2 cups) olive oil
or other salad oil
4 cloves garlic
4 ounces Roquefort or blue cheese
¼ cup vinegar
3 tablespoons sugar
1 tablespoon salt
½ teaspoon pepper
4 or 5 drops Worcestershire

An electric blender is used in making this Roquefort cheese dressing.

Add a small amount of oil to the garlic in the blender, and blend at high speed to mix well. Add about 2 ounces of the cheese and blend for a short time. Then add enough more oil to make 1 pint of dressing. Add oil in small amounts, blending well after each addition. Break the remaining along with remaining ingredients. Place in the refrigerator for several hours or overnight. Makes about 2½ cups dressing.

Three-Cheese Dressing

¼ pound blue cheese
1 large package (8 oz.) cream cheese
4 tablespoons grated Sap
Sago cheese
½ teaspoon tarragon
1 teaspoon salt
¼ teaspoon pepper
½ clove garlic, mashed
About ½ cup milk

This blue cheese dressing has an intriguing extra flavor contributed by Sap Sago cheese. The cream cheese blends the ingredients into a smooth dressing that is delicious on tossed green salads and other vegetable salads.

Using the small bowl of your electric mixer, mix together the blue cheese, cream cheese, and Sap Sago cheese until well blended. Add the tarragon, salt, pepper, and garlic purée. Gradually beat in milk until the dressing is the consistency of medium-thick cream. Use immediately, or cover and refrigerate to use later. Makes about 3 cups dressing.

Photo Guide to Salad Making

LEAF LETTUCE—Delicate taste; very tender, fragile leaves, lightweight, closely crinkled

ROMAINE (Cos)—Brittle-crisp, somewhat fibrous, clean-tearing; spicy-mild and juicy

AUSTRALIAN (Oak Leaf, Salad Bowl)—Mellow flavor, slight bite; soft, suede-like leaf

CHICORY (Curly Endive)—Wiry, sharply feathered, wispy leaf; sprightly, rather bitter flavor

WATERCRESS—Lively and spicy sweetness; sharp and biting; fragile, petal-like leaves

BUTTER (Boston, Butterhead) —Mild, almost tasteless; pliable soft leaf; velvety texture

HEAD (Iceberg, Los Angeles Market)—Unexcelled crispness; icy bite; watery taste

BELGIAN ENDIVE (French)— Lively taste: rich, mildly acrid; waxen, crunchy spears

ESCAROLE (Broad Leaf Endive) —Sharp, slightly bitter; rough textured, wiry, leathery leaf

134

A TEMPTING ARRAY *of salad greens is available in today's markets. Nine of the major kinds are shown here. For some salads, you'll want to use a single kind; but when little or nothing is added to the greens, a combination of two or more greens will give contrast in colors, flavors, and textures.*

GREEN ONIONS—Appetizing aroma, sweet-onion piquancy

FENNEL (Anise)—Use stalk and feathery top; licorice sweetness

LEEKS—Robust, strong aroma; a mild, sweet, oniony flavor

CELERY TOPS—Fragile tufts; nutty, spicy; sweet pungency

DANDELION GREENS—Thin, arrowy leaf; tart-bitter taste

MUSTARD GREENS—Young, fully frilled leaves; peppery-bitter

CHIVES—Refined onion qualities; dainty and refreshing fragrance

BEET TOPS—Young, firm leaves; mildly sour, salty

SPINACH—Tender young leaves; sharp edges; clean, "green" taste

NASTURTIUM LEAVES—Peppery, somewhat like watercress

MINT—Fruity, refreshingly sweet scent; fuzzy leaves

PARSLEY—Acid-sweet, fresh, ferny leafed, slightly tough

"ACCESSORY" GREENS *add an element of surprise and interest to a salad. The twelve above are by no means an exhaustive collection. A tossed green salad might include such ingredients as collards, sorrel, Bok Choy (Chinese chard), Chinese cabbage, or herbs fresh from the garden.*

135

FOR THIS MIXED GREEN SALAD, *we selected a variety of greens: romaine, butterhead, red-edge* Prize Head, chicory, avocado slices for garnish. Toss torn greens with a distinctive dressing.

VEGETABLE SALAD *shown here combines kidney beans; cooked and chilled peas, asparagus, beans; quartered tomatoes. Salad is arranged in lettuce cups, served with Thousand Island dressing.*

FULL-MEAL SALAD: *Shrimp, sliced celery, chopped egg, mixed with salad dressing or mayonnaise, lemon juice, salt, pepper, celery seed, shredded lettuce, egg slices, tomato, green pepper.*

GREEN SALAD, SMORGASBORD STYLE *(page 14)*
presents colorful picture. Bowl of lettuce includes
romaine, leaf, Australian, Belgian endive, chicory.
Other ingredients are served separately, to be
sprinkled on individual servings. Toss greens with
Piquant Dressing (page 125) just before serving.

INGREDIENTS FOR CAESAR SALAD *(page 20) are shown here. This salad is invariably tossed at the table where guests can watch the host or hostess season and mix the greens. Crisp and flavorful romaine leaves, torn into large pieces, always form the background of a Caesar Salad.*

GRAPEFRUIT SECTIONS *and avocado slices arranged in an alternating pattern on a crisp bed of curly endive, are pleasing to the eye.*

GREEN GODDESS SALAD *(page 20), with a lobster garnish, is an especially colorful and rich version of plain green salad. The creamy dressing may be used on many salads, both light and hearty.*

A SALAD LUNCHEON, *served buffet-style in the garden, is an ideal way to entertain, as most of the preparations can be made the night before. Ingredients can be prepared and refrigerated in separate containers for combining the next day. Lettuce can be washed, wrapped in damp towels, and stored in the refrigerator.*

139

REMOVE CORE *from a large, firm head of lettuce; hollow out a hole 5 inches deep in center of head.*

COLOR-FLECKED *filling for iceberg lettuce: Combine 3-oz. package cream cheese with 3 tablespoons mayonnaise; 2 tablespoons each grated carrot, chopped tomato; 1 tablespoon each chopped green pepper, pimiento, onion; salt, paprika, pepper.*

STUFF WITH *cream cheese filling; wrap with aluminum foil and chill for 6 hours. Slice in crosswise slices; serve on chop plate with olives and radishes mounded in center.*

WEDGES OF *iceberg lettuce are served with a Thousand Island Dressing to which chopped beets were added for color interest.*

MINCED VEGETABLE DRESSING *(page 126) ideally complements sliced tomatoes, cucumbers. This dressing is also good on lettuce wedges.*

Anchovies
Sardines

Artichoke Hearts
Pickled Mushrooms

Lemons

Salt & Pepper

Mayonnaise

Pickled Onions
Beets

Chopped Egg

Flat Bread
French Bread
Rye Wafers
Rye Bread

Jellied Tongue
Turkey, Ham
Salami, Beef

Cream Cheese
Cheddar Cheese
Blue Cheese
Swiss Cheese
Parmesan Cheese

Ripe Olives

Oil & Vinegar

Iceberg Lettuce

Prize Head Lettuce

Escarole

Chicory

Romaine

Carrots
Tomatoes
Onions
Cauliflower
Radishes

Garlic Croutons

Shrimp

Toasted Almonds

Edible-Pod Peas

Green Olives

Crumbled Bacon

Smoked Salmon

Crab

SALAD BUFFET *is fun to assemble and fun for the guests. The picture above doesn't begin to show all of the foods which could go on the buffet table. In addition to the mayonnaise and the cruets of oil and vinegar, you might set on the table a variety of dressings and condiments. You might add toasted sesame seeds, slivered bologna, smoked turkey, smoked oyster bits, or flaked tuna to the accompaniments. Vegetable possibilities are almost unlimited, and you can branch out into fruit salads, too.*

142 ANTIPASTO SALAD *(page 18) is arranged on base of shredded romaine and chicory. Australian leaf lettuce forms border. Strips of antipasto ingredients* are tuna chunks, pimiento strips, chopped green onion, radish slices, chopped egg yolks and whites, green olive slices, anchovy fillets, chopped parsley.

MUSHROOM AND LIMA BEAN *salad (page 59) is heaped in a large casserole lined with romaine leaves. Salad is seasoned with Italian flavors.*

WEDGES *of hard-cooked eggs decorate Dilled Green Pea Salad (page 56). Toasted cornbread squares are a delicious accompaniment.*

LEMON SLAW *(page 61) is colorful, and it tastes as good as it looks. Fresh lemon juice, plus a little grated lemon peel, gives the dressing a refreshing tang.*

COBB SALAD (*page 82*) *is a taste surprise. Rich with chicken, tomatoes, hard-cooked eggs, Roquefort cheese, and avocados, it is a meal in itself.*

CRANBERRY BEANS *are the main ingredient in this robust salad which would be a good choice for a winter luncheon. The recipe appears on page 58. As accompaniments, you might serve bouillon, bran muffins, an assortment of cheeses, and a platter of cold sliced meat loaf or other cold meats.*

MUSHROOM-OLIVE SALAD *(page 64) is dressed with a garlic-flavored dressing. Celery, onions, and parsley give added texture contrasts.*

ORANGE AND CUCUMBER *slices are tucked among leaves of butter lettuce, and overlapping onion rings decorate the top. Recipe on page 21.*

THREE COLORFUL PARTY SALADS: *Fruits frozen in Sherry cream base (page 108); avocados with pears and pineapple (page 29); tomato with poached oyster and anchovy sauce (page 86).*

CHICKEN SALAD PIQUANT *(page 78) has a flavorful low-calorie dressing that will please weight watchers—only about 2 calories per tablespoon.*

CHICKEN AND AVOCADO TOSTADO DE LUXE *(page 80) served on a Mexican plate, presents a colorful picture. Avocado slices radiate above crisp tortilla, shredded lettuce, hot chili bean sauce, sliced chicken.*

SHRIMP SALAD WITH LEMON DRESSING *(page 90) is served on water cress, and embellished with tiny pickled beets and bright deviled eggs. Shrimp are chilled in ice cubes before serving.*

GRAPEFRUIT SEGMENTS *alternate with papaya slices on a bed of crisp iceberg lettuce and water cress. Sliced hearts of palm and chopped ripe olives* embellish this buffet salad. Ingredients used: 1 large grapefruit, 1 papaya, 1 can (14 oz.) hearts of palm, and 12 pitted ripe olives.

TO MAKE GRAPEFRUIT SEGMENTS, *peel grapefruit down to meat in circular fashion, removing all of the outer skin and inside membrane.*

SLIP KNIFE *down one side of dividing membrane, then continue along the membrane on the other side of segment so fruit drops out.*

FRUIT PLATE OF *papaya, orange, banana, and pine-apple slices is topped with Papaya Seed Dressing (page 124). Papaya seeds taste a little like capers, substitute beautifully for poppy seeds in this dressing.*

PEAR SLICER *cuts papaya fast. Remove blossom end from small papaya; push slicer through; peel with potato peeler.*

To prepare half papaya, *scoop out seeds with a teaspoon. They're easy to remove, as they tend to cling together.*

Half papaya, *served with a wedge of either lemon or lime, is a popular eye-opener in tropical countries. Papaya is ripe when it's yellow with only a few flecks of green.*

Papaya, *oranges, and avocados, drenched in an onion-flecked, red chili dressing (page 38) have marinated earlier in this same mixture.*

Star-shaped cavity *in papaya is different from the round center in most melons. Stuff with cream cheese mixture (page 39), then slice.*

149

HAM AND CHEESE RICE SALAD (page 95) is served in a casserole. It has the heartiness of an oven-baked casserole, but it is served crisp and cold. The Swiss cheese, ham, and dill are a mellow blend of flavors.

AVOCADO HALVES, filled with mandarin oranges and arranged on a bed of curly endive, are a good first course for a meal (see page 31).

FRUIT AND COTTAGE CHEESE *salad in romaine leaves (page 25) has a garnish of cantaloupe and strawberries. It is served with an unusual mint-flavored dressing.*

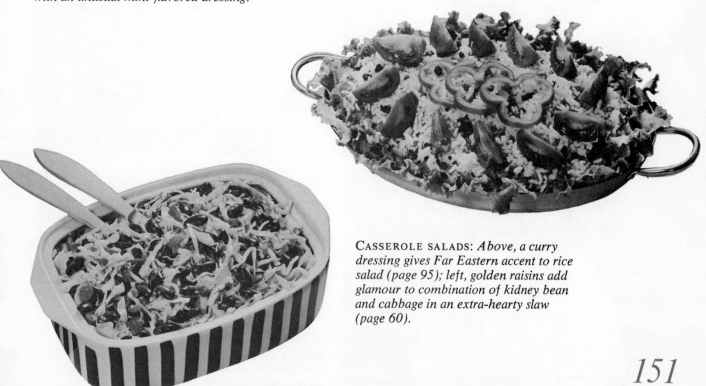

CASSEROLE SALADS: *Above, a curry dressing gives Far Eastern accent to rice salad (page 95); left, golden raisins add glamour to combination of kidney bean and cabbage in an extra-hearty slaw (page 60).*

151

FROSTED SALMON MOUSSE (page 115) is a delicious luncheon entreé. The molded salmon salad is flecked with sliced ripe olives, and frosted with a pale green avocado-sour cream mixture.

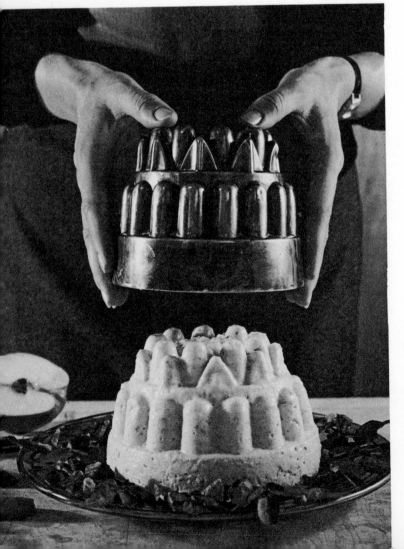

TOMATO ASPIC RING, filled with avocado cubes which were sprinkled with salt and lemon juice, and surrounded by deviled hard-cooked eggs, could be the entire menu for a company luncheon. Serve it with French dressing to which chopped chives have been added.

WASHINGTON APPLE SALAD (page 101) is delicate and rather sweet. Cottage cheese and evaporated milk substitute for the more typical cream cheese and whipping cream.

LIME-LEMON-ORANGE LAYERED SALAD *(page 106) is an unusual combination of fruits and vegetables, with a sour cream layer in the center. It is garnished with pineapple chunks, green-colored maraschino cherries, and halved bananas coated with chopped peanuts.*

DOUBLE-DECKER *Pineapple-Cherry Salad (page 108) has a thin layer of cream cheese sandwiched between the two fruit-flavored layers. Mandarin oranges and cream cheese balls rolled in coconut provide a flavorful garnish.*

153

CHEESE-FILLED *fresh pineapple is cut in slices for serving. Cheese is softened with a little cream and mixed with nut meats and sliced maraschino cherries.*

TO PREPARE *pineapple, remove top and bottom; remove rind and cut out any remaining eyes. Use cylinder from cooky press to remove core.*

PACK CREAM CHEESE *mixture into hollow center; wrap in waxed paper and chill thoroughly. Cut into thick slices; serve on leaves or greens.*

154

SWEET DARK CHERRIES, *coarsely chopped pecans, and sliced pimiento-stuffed olives are molded in orange-flavored gelatin (page 103).*

AVOCADO HALF *filled with hot buttered popcorn (page 28) is a conversation piece. Serve it on a bed of lettuce, and sprinkle with rum or lemon juice.*

ORANGE COTTAGE CHEESE *tops pineapple slices (page 44) for an attractive buffet salad plate. Dressing is served in hollowed-out pineapple shell.*

SLICES *of hard-cooked eggs decorate aspic shell for Ham and Tongue Aspic (page 112). Eggs are dipped in aspic, then attached to sides of mold.*

MELON MOLD WITH CHERRIES (page 103), turned out on a bed of fresh mint, is garnished with cantaloupe balls. Fruits used in the molded salad are cantaloupe, Bing cherries, and pineapple. Cherry juice colors the gelatin base deep purple, and pineapple juice gives it added flavor.

TO MAKE melon mold shown above and described on page 103, first dissolve lemon-flavored gelatin in hot pineapple juice. Add cherry juice; chill.

PEEL cantaloupe, cut into cubes, and place in bottom of mold. Add pineapple and cherries to chilled gelatin and pour over cantaloupe cubes.

156

AVOCADO AND TOMATO SALAD *(page 102) looks festive when you mold it in a fluted mold and garnish it with cherry tomatoes, lemon wedges, and* *avocado slices. To make it, you mold an avocado-sour cream aspic on top of a tomato aspic. Serve it with sliced smoked salmon for a summer luncheon.*

ORANGE, *pineapple, and apricot layers form this eye-catching salad. Salted almonds fill the center of the ring, and prunes stuffed with mandarin oranges surround it. Recipe on page 107.*

Index

Photographs in this book are by the following photographers: Clyde
Childress, Glenn Christiansen, Robert Cox, Blair Stapp, Darrow Watt.